Japanese Americans

Other Titles in This Series

Westview Special Studies in Contemporary Social Issues

Japanese Americans:
Changing Patterns of Ethnic Affiliation
Over Three Generations

Darrel Montero

Despite many social injustices, Japanese Americans are one of the most socioeconomically successful ethnic groups in the United States, having the highest median educational level among both nonwhite and white groups, a median income exceeding that of white Americans, and greater likelihood of being employed as professionals than are members of the society as a whole. Given each succeeding generation's increasing rate of assimilation into U.S. society, with its concomitant impact upon ethnic ties and affiliation, the author asks whether or not a distinct Japanese community can be maintained into the fourth generation.

This study, which employs a national sample of three generations of Japanese Americans, is the largest of its kind ever undertaken. The volume systematically analyzes the socioeconomic adaptation of the Japanese to U.S. society and develops a sociohistorical model that explains the unfolding of the assimilation process for this three-generational sample of Japanese Americans.

Darrel Montero, who received his Ph.D. in sociology at the University of California, Los Angeles, is associate professor and director of the Urban Ethnic Research Program, Arizona State University.

Japanese Americans:
Changing Patterns of Ethnic Affiliation Over Three Generations

Darrel Montero

Westview Press / Boulder, Colorado

Westview Special Studies in Contemporary Social Issues

Copyright © 1980 by Westview Press, Inc.

Published in 1980 in the United States of America by
Westview Press, Inc.
5500 Central Avenue
Boulder, Colorado 80301
Frederick A. Praeger, Publisher

Library of Congress Cataloging in Publication Data
Montero, Darrel.
Japanese Americans.
(Westview special studies in contemporary social issues)
Bibliography: p.
1. Japanese Americans—Ethnic identity. 2. Japanese Americans—Social conditions. I. Title.
E184.J3M6   301.45'19'56073   79-9428
ISBN 0-89158-595-8

Printed and bound in the United States of America

For Mother and Dad, and Tara and David

Contents

Tables and Figures

Preface

My interest in the study of Japanese Americans was first sparked during my years as a graduate student in sociology at the University of California, Los Angeles (UCLA), when I became a member of the Japanese American Research Project (JARP). As director of research on that project, my work made me acutely aware of the discrimination and hardship the Japanese have faced in America, and the socioeconomic advances they have achieved despite the difficulties they faced. The story of the Japanese in America is one of remarkable endurance and pride. There is much to be learned from their struggles and painstaking progress, and I am ever grateful for the opportunity I have had to know them better.

The Japanese American Citizens' League initiated the study upon which this volume is based, and grants were contributed by that organization, the Carnegie Corporation, and the National Institute of Mental Health (Grant No. 5 R01 MH12780-04). Computer time was provided by UCLA and by the Computer Science Center at the University of Maryland, College Park.

Members of the Japanese American Citizens' League also gave emotional support and practical day-to-day assistance throughout the decade or more of the project's history. Specifically, I thank Shigeo Wakamatsu (chairman of the League's History Committee), Mike Masaoka, Frank Chuman, and the late Joe Grant Masaoka (manager of the project).

Many individuals worked on the project during its ten-year duration, and their unique contributions and unfailing devotion added immeasurably to its successful completion. I gratefully acknowledge:

T. Scott Miyakawa, who initiated the research;

John Modell, who guided the project during its early years; and Gregory Stone and Gladys Stone, who also made major contributions;

Robert A. Wilson, who was a constant source of historical information;

Yasuo Sakata, whose numerous contributions included the preparation of the initial listing from which the first-generation sample was drawn;

Michael Walton, Bruce Huffman, and the late Leo G. Reeder (former director of UCLA's Survey Research Center), who supervised the processing and coding of the three-generation data; Michael Edlen, Donald M. Long, Robert Rhodes, Michael Rudd, and Michael Waite, whose computer programming and analytic skills simplified my task;

Roger Girod, Harry H. L. Kitano, S. Frank Miyamoto, Raymond J. Murphy, Tomatsu Shibutani, and Ralph H. Turner, who were the project advisors and consultants;

Joyce Lazar and Lorraine B. Torres, project officers at the National Institute of Mental Health;

Edna Bonacich, research associate of the Japanese American Research Project, for her wise counsel and for her generosity in sharing the related methodological materials presented in Chapter 3;

And especially Gene N. Levine, who was principal investigator of the project and who, as my teacher and friend, guided my studies during my graduate years and stimulated my intellecutal curiosity and enthusiasm for social research.

This volume has evolved from my doctoral dissertation in sociology at UCLA. In that initial effort I was aided immeasurably by Kenneth D. Bailey, Robert A. Wilson, and (again) Gene N. Levine. Subsequently, all or parts of the manuscript have been read by Edna Bonacich, Andrew Cherlin, Marvin Dawkins, Stanford M. Lyman, Tara McLaughlin, Patricia Rathbun, R. A. Schermerhorn, Frank Stratford, Judith Treas, and Robin M. Williams, Jr. Their comments and suggestions I received gratefully, and wherever possible I tried to comply with their suggested revisions. Any errors or omissions, of course, are entirely my own.

I thank Claudia Burns and Chris Turner for their assistance in data processing, and Kay Huke and Nancy Clancy for their good nature while preparing the manuscript for publication.

I also thank the editorial department at Westview Press: Lynne C. Rienner, Associate Publisher, and Miriam Gilbert, Managing Editor, for encouraging me to undertake the project, as well as the kindness they have shown me throughout the manuscript's many revisions; Jeanne E. Remington, Marjorie J. DeFries, and Debra Balducci for their expert and prompt processing of the manuscript.

I wish to express my special appreciation to my friend and colleague Judith McDowell, Research Associate with the University of Maryland's Urban Ethnic Research Program. Judy's careful review and critique of the manuscript greatly improved it and insured that the volume would be completed on schedule. Equally important are her keen intellect and good nature that made the enterprise enjoyable.

Finally, I thank my parents, who are a constant source of inspiration and support, and my wife, Tara, whose intellectual spirit and encouragement made the volume possible.

Darrel Montero
Tempe, Arizona

1
Background to the Study of the Japanese American Community

From the earliest contacts between the United States and Japan, Americans have viewed the people of the East as both anomalous and enigmatic. Many features of the Japanese have contributed to this interpretation. These include, inter alia, a seemingly impassive demeanor, racial and ethnic pride and cohesiveness, and, recently and most notable, astounding and rapid economic achievements.

Upon the first arrival of a Japanese embassy to the United States in 1860, a San Francisco newspaper, the *Daily Alta Californian*, reported with awe upon their manners:

> Every beholder was struck with the self-possessed demeanor of the Japanese. Though the scenes which now met their gaze must have been of the most intense interest for novelty, they seemed to consider this display as due the august position they held under their Emperor and not one of them, by sign or word, evidenced either surprise or admiration.[1]

After tens of thousands of Japanese had entered the country as immigrants, many Americans became accustomed to their appearance and mannerisms; however, other more fundamental characteristics of this group drew their attention. For example, in a 1921 survey of some seven American immigrant groups, Robert Park observed that "the Japanese are the most efficiently and completely organized among the immigrant groups."[2]

Japanese immigrants to the United States and their descendants have more recently received national attention for their social and economic achievements. One thesis that has been expressed in sociological literature contends that certain cultures

1

have a "need for achievement" that manifests itself with an emphasis on thrift, hard work, and deferred gratification.[3] This thesis, it appears, would most aptly apply to the Japanese. William Petersen, for example, contends that through hard work, patience, and perseverance Japanese Americans have pulled themselves up by their bootstraps.[4] Several studies have attempted to unearth the causes of the Japanese Americans' considerable socioeconomic gains.[5] The central concern of this study is to examine one aspect of the gains made by this remarkable American minority. We are concerned with the effects on the quality of the ethnic community of its members' socioeconomic advance. Will the strides made by the Japanese Americans prove to be functional or dysfunctional with regard to the continuance of close intragroup ties?

To the social scientist, Japanese Americans present a singular history that has included sporadic immigration patterns, racial persecution, and, despite these, substantial socioeconomic achievement. The immigrant Japanese were confronted with an entirely foreign culture, including language, food, religion, and social system. White Americans noted the differences between themselves and the Japanese in skin color and physique, and concluded that the newcomers were completely unassimilable into the mainstream of society.[6] This minority has been subjected to a series of social injustices, including the 1907/1908 Gentlemen's Agreement, the Alien Land Laws of 1913 and 1920, and World War II relocation; yet, Japanese Americans are one of the most successful ethnic groups in the United States.

Japanese Americans have the highest median years of education among both nonwhite and white groups (Table 1.1). Furthermore, according to the 1970 Census, they have a median family income of $13,542, nearly $4,000 more than that of the average U.S. family (Table 1.2). Similarly, Table 1.3 indicates that in the area of occupational achievement Japanese Americans are much more likely to be employed as professionals than the U.S. population as a whole: in 1970, 21 percent of the Japanese population, as compared with only 14 percent of the total U.S. population, were professionals.

It is important to note, however, that many Japanese Americans are concerned that too much emphasis is being placed

Table 1.1

Median Number of School Years Completed for
White and Nonwhite Populations[a]

Total	White	Black	Indian	Chinese	Japanese	Filipino
12.0	12.1	9.8	9.8	12.4	12.5	12.2

[a]Source: U. S. Bureau of the Census (1973a, 1973b, 1973c, 1973d).

Table 1.2

Income Characteristics of the U.S.
Total Population and Asian Americans, 1970[a]

Total U.S.	Japanese	Chinese	Filipino
$9,590	$13,542	$10,610	$9,318

[a]Note: Figures represent median family income.

Source: U.S. Department of Health, Education, and Welfare (1974:105).

Table 1.3

Comparison of Occupational Distribution of Nisei Sample
with Total U.S. and Total Japanese American Population

	Nisei Sample (1967)	Japanese Americans 1960 (a)	U.S. 1960 (b)	U.S. 1970 (c)	Japanese Americans 1970 (d)
Professional, Technical, and Kindred Workers	32%	19%	10%	14%	21%
Managers, Officials, Proprietors, excluding Farm	20	10	11	11	12
Clerical, Sales, and Kindred Workers	11	12	14	14	15
Farmers, Farm Managers, Farm Laborers and Foremen	14	26	8	5	5
Craftsmen, Foremen, Operatives, and Kindred	12	21	42	41	30
Service Workers, and Laborers, excluding Farm	11	12	14	15	17
	(1998)	(62,848)	(43,562,353)		(147,054)
				(47,730,661)	

Note: Figures derived from the following: Japanese American
    Males 14+ years (excluding residents of Hawaii) in 1960
    Census, U.S. Males 14+ years in 1960 Census, U.S. Males
    16+ years in 1970 Census, and Japanese American Males 16+
    years in 1970 Census.

(a) U.S. Bureau of the Census (1963a: 108,110).
(b) U.S. Bureau of the Census (1963c: Table 1).
(c) U.S. Bureau of the Census (1972: Table 1).
(d) U.S. Bureau of the Census (1973d).

upon the socioeconomic success of this ethnic minority, when in fact many of its members are still trying hard to overcome racial and economic discrimination.[7] The label of success has made society at large blind to the difficulties that many Japanese Americans face. Kitano has pointed out that those Japanese who are employed in administrative and executive positions are most likely to live east of the Mississippi River.[8] On the West Coast, where the greatest concentration of Japanese Americans reside, this minority group continues to perceive both blatant and subtle discrimination from the white majority.

Consider that first generation Japanese Americans were barred from owning land for decades under the 1913 California Land Law, and that some 110,000 Japanese Americans who lived in the three Pacific Coast states were interned during World War II under Executive Order 9066. With all their disadvantages, disruptions, and discouragements, the group has indeed overcome great obstacles. The determinants of this success invite delineation and interpretation. It is not the Japanese American immigration and early social history in the United States that require analysis, since these have been examined in numerous works.[9] Rather, it is the social development of this group that invites further examination — the processes and the mechanisms of their adaptation to American culture.

We note from Table 1.4 that by 1970 there were some 591,290 Japanese Americans in the United States, and that more than one-third of these lived in Hawaii. Most of the earliest Japanese Americans came to the United States as sojourners. They fled no political horrors or religious persecution; rather, they came to make tidy sums of money, then to return to their native land. But in fact the greater the success they achieved here, the more difficult it became to give up their successful enterprises. Being family-oriented, some had brought wives and children with them. Others waited to become financially and geographically established before sending for fiancées waiting at home. Still others sent for "picture" or "mail-order" brides as the only way to start a family unit in a land of few eligible Japanese females.[10] With the passage of time, growing families and a measure of financial security made it extremely difficult to pull up stakes and return to a now distant homeland. Those who did return to Japan found that social and economic conditions had changed to such an

Table 1.4

United States

Population of Chinese, Japanese, and Filipino

Census Year	Chinese			Japanese			Filipino		
	Mainland	Hawaii	Total	Mainland	Hawaii	Total	Mainland	Hawaii	Total
1860	34,933								
1870	63,199								
1880	105,465			148					
1890	107,488	16,752	124,240	2,039					
1900	89,863	25,767	115,630	24,326	61,111	85,437			
1910	71,531	21,674	93,205	72,157	79,675	151,832	160	2,361	2,521
1920	61,639	23,507	85,146	111,010	109,274	220,284	5,603	21,031	26,634
1930	74,954	27,179	102,133	138,834	139,631	278,465	45,208	63,052	108,260
1940	77,504	28,774	106,278	126,947	157,905	284,852	45,563	52,569	98,132
1950	117,629	32,376	150,005	141,768	184,598	326,366	61,636	61,062	122,698
1960	199,095	38,197	237,292	260,877	203,455	464,332	106,424	69,070	175,494
1970	383,023	52,039	435,062	373,983	217,307	591,290	249,145	93,915	343,060

Note: Based on 1960 and 1970 reports of the Bureau of the Census and on Lind (1967). No entry indicates that data were unavailable.

extent that it had become very difficult to eke out a living in Japan. Their reports quickly became widespread and deterred other Japanese from returning to the land of their ancestors.

How have the Japanese fared in the face of hardship, prejudice, and the discrimination encountered throughout the ordeals of World War II? The record says: with distinction. When compared with other ethnic minorities, the Japanese have an extremely low incidence of mental illness, crime, delinquency, suicide, and imprisonment.[11] As we have noted, census data reveal that the Japanese Americans outperform all other nonwhite and all white subpopulations in educational attainments with a median of 12.5 school years completed. This is half a year higher than the nation as a whole and almost three years higher than Blacks and Indians. On almost all other measures of socio-economic and cultural success (e.g., occupational status and financial prosperity), the Japanese have also made great strides.[12]

One major explanation for these achievements has been advanced by Miyamoto, Light, and others.[13] Essentially, these authors have stressed the importance of the supportiveness and cohesiveness of the ethnic community for its members' success and welfare. In his comparative study of Blacks, Chinese, and Japanese Americans, Light found that the *kenjinkai* (social organizations based on prefectural origins of immigrants) and *tanomoshi* (credit associations) helped to give Japanese Americans institutional support by pooling their limited capital to establish and to maintain small businesses and farms. There is substantial evidence that the considerable success of Japanese Americans is attributable to community organization and solidarity.[14]

The Japanese are the only ethnic group to emphasize geogenerational distinctions by a separate nomenclature and a belief in the unique character structure of each generational group.[15] The *Issei* (first generation), *Nisei* (second generation), and *Sansei* (third generation) became reference groups for individual Japanese Americans, each generation establishing its own rules of status and definitions of boundaries. Reinforced by their own generational identity, members of each group sought to enforce some degree of conformity within that particular generation.[16] According to Lyman the generational identity was a kind of cement that really gave cohesiveness to the Japanese.[17] The origins of cohesiveness and social solidarity in the Japanese American community are also well documented by Miyamoto and Kitano.[18]

It is not our intent to elaborate further upon the well-known aspect of the Japanese American people just described. Instead, as noted, we speculate on the survival and development of the ethnic community during a period when its members have been advancing socioeconomically to a striking degree. Part of the answer may lie in the Japanese Americans' ability to establish themselves while managing to retain many important traditions. We have found that many minority groups have by and large fared less well in preserving the essentials of their culture.

In what way has the achievement of an improved economic status affected the value system of this minority group?[19] Does the Japanese Americans' success cause a measurable degree of disengagement from the ethnic community? That is, in the course of becoming successful, does one leave the social or geographical confines of his ethnic community either by choice or circumstance? Does departure from the community smooth the road to success? In short, we inquire into the interrelationship between socioeconomic success and the continued cohesiveness of the community. We are particularly interested in examining the question of whether or not socioeconomic mobility leads to cultural and structural assimilation among the Japanese Americans.

Over two decades ago in a review of the literature, Ianni observed that most studies of the acculturation of American ethnic groups have indicated some positive relationship between acculturation and social mobility.[20] While few of these studies were explicitly oriented to measuring social mobility, they usually contained some reference to an observation by the field worker that the ethnic group member with higher social status in the general community also tends to be more acculturated.[21] In Yankee city, for example, the least acculturated ethnic groups and the least acculturated members within the various groups are also characterized by low social status.[22] Numerous studies of Mexican-American groups have described the low social status and relatively slight acculturation of these groups while pointing to the higher degree of acculturation of the upwardly mobile Mexican American.[23] A similar relationship between social mobility

and acculturation has been described among the Greeks, the
Irish, the Italians, and the Jews.[24]

What chance, then, do Japanese Americans have to maintain
their ethnic boundaries in confrontation with the juggernaut of
mainstream American culture that they aspire to enter, even if
that aspiration is limited to a desire for economic security and success? With data from a three-generational, national sample of
Japanese Americans, we approach our problem by focusing upon
the second-generation Japanese Americans, the Nisei. As we see
below, it is they and not their parents (the Issei) or their children
(the Sansei) who have produced the central themes of the
Japanese experience in the United States.

We are, of course, concerned with the relevance of our findings
on the Japanese for the experiences of other ethnic groups in the
United States — for example, Blacks and Chicanos. When they,
too, will have gained notable socioeconomic achievements, will
these groups undergo geographic dispersion and total assimilation? The answer to this question has important implications
for the frequently debated issue of assimilation versus pluralism
as discussed by Gordon, and Glazer and Moynihan.[25] We can
further inquire whether or not the pluralistic model of ethnic
adaptation is possible if the most upwardly mobile leave the social
and geographic confines of the group. Have the successful Nisei
and Sansei had to leave what they may have subjectively considered to be the suffocation of their community in order to follow
their callings, or is the reverse true? Although not living in the
geographical confines of their original ethnic communities, some
Nisei and Sansei may maintain an important interaction with
their families and communities. And even in their physical
absence, they may retain ethnic affiliations (e.g., membership in
a national ethnic organization), although the quality and saliency
of the ties may be weakened.

We focus, then, on the relationship between socioeconomic
success and level of immersion in the Nisei and Sansei ethnic
community. The major independent variables are age, sex, occupation, and education. Dependent variables are composed of
an interlocking set of measures of degree of Nisei and Sansei community affiliation and immersion. They include (1) neighborhood
ethnicity, (2) indicators of visiting patterns with relatives in the

community, (3) ethnic composition of voluntary associations, (4) friends' ethnicity, and (5) spouse ethnicity.

Notes

1. Lewis Bush, *77 Samurai*, p. 132. Cited in Stanford M. Lyman, *The Asian in the West*, p. 81. Based on the original manuscript in Japanese by Itsuro Hattori. Bush does not give the date of this newspaper article. It would appear to be April 2, 1860.

2. Robert E. Park and Herbert A. Miller, *Old World Traits Transplanted*, p. 168.

3. Bernard C. Rosen, "Race, Ethnicity, and the Achievement Syndrome."

4. William Petersen, *Japanese Americans*.

5. For reviews of findings, see Leonard Bloom and Ruth Reimer, *Removal and Return*; Gene N. Levine and Darrel Montero, "Socioeconomic Mobility among Three Generations of Japanese Americans"; Ivan H. Light, *Ethnic Enterprise in America*; Patricia A. Roos, "Questioning the Stereotypes"; Calvin E. Schmid and Charles E. Nobbe, "Socioeconomic Differentials among Non-White Races"; A. J. Schwartz, *Traditional Values and Contemporary Achievement of Japanese American Pupils*; A. J. Schwartz, idem, "The Culturally Advantaged"; Stanley Sue and Harry H. L. Kitano, eds., "Asian Americans"; and Barbara F. Varon, "The Japanese Americans."

6. Dennis Ogawa, *From Japs to Japanese*, p. 9.

7. Robert C. Toth, "Japanese in U.S. Outdo Horatio Alger."

8. Harry H. L. Kitano, *Race Relations*.

9. For reviews of findings, see Hilary Conroy and T. Scott Miyakawa, eds., *East across the Pacific;* Roger Daniels, *The Politics of Prejudice;* Y. Ichihashi, *Japanese in the United States;* T. Scott Miyakawa and Yasuo Sakata, "Japan in Dislocation and Emigration"; John Modell, *The Economics and Politics of Racial Accommodation*; and Y. Sakata, "Japanese Immigration to the United States."

10. Ichihashi, *Japanese in the United States*.

11. Harry H. L. Kitano, *Japanese Americans*; and Harry H. L. Kitano, *Japanese Americans*, 2nd ed.

12. Levine and Montero, "Socioeconomic Mobility among Three Generations of Japanese Americans"; and Petersen, *Japanese Americans*.

13. S. Frank Miyamoto, "Social Solidarity among the Japanese in Seattle"; and Light, *Ethnic Enterprise in America*.

14. Light, *Ethnic Enterprise in America*.

15. Stanford M. Lyman, *The Asian in North America,* p. 121.

16. Christie Kiefer, *Changing Cultures, Changing Lives*, p. 99.

17. Lyman, *The Asian in North America*, p. 281.

18. Miyamoto, "Social Solidarity among the Japanese in Seattle"; and Kitano, *Japanese Americans*.

19. Edna M. Bonacich, "A Theory of Middleman Minorities."

20. Francis A. J. Ianni, "Residential and Occupational Mobility as Indices of the Acculturation of an Ethnic Group."

21. Melford E. Spiro, "The Acculturation of American Ethnic Groups."

22. W. Lloyd Warner and Leo Srole, *The Social Systems of American Ethnic Groups.*

23. For reviews of findings, see George C. Barker, "Social Functions of Language in a Mexican-American Community"; Norman D. Humphrey, "The Detroit Mexican Immigrant and Naturalization"; Donovan Senter and Florence Hawley, "The Grammar School as the Basic Acculturating Influence for Native New Mexicans"; and James B. Watson and Julian Samora, "Subordinate Leadership in a Bicultural Community."

24. See Henry Pratt Fairchild, *Greek Immigration to the United States*; Carl Wittke, *The Irish in America*; Irvin L. Child, *Italian or American*; Francis A. J. Ianni, "The Acculturation of the Italo-Americans in Norristown, Pennsylvania"; Jerome K. Myers, "The Differential Time Factor in Assimilation"; William Foote Whyte, *Street Corner Society*; and Albert I. Gordon, *Jews in Transition*.

25. Milton Gordon, *Assimilation in American Life*; Milton Gordon, "Toward a General Theory of Racial and Ethnic Group Relations"; and Nathan Glazer and Daniel P. Moynihan, *Beyond the Melting Pot*.

2
Structure and Process: The Nature of the Japanese American Community

The concept of community has been utilized by many social scientists in understanding social life. It has been described on the one hand as a positive force, an intricate network of social mechanisms that binds human groups together. According to this view, community provides a structured setting that gives meaning to people's lives by providing and reinforcing the dominant values and norms of the group. Some observers note that without these social guidelines anarchy would prevail, and human groups as we now know them would cease to exist.

A radical perspective, on the other hand, might lead us to argue that although mores and norms play a functional role in maintaining the structure and process of human groups, they may serve, beyond a certain point, to stifle individual potential. They may become dysfunctional, for example, by perpetuating a rigid system of social stratification. Another example of the dysfunctional elements of norms might be the imposition of unduly restrictive sexual standards that are practiced with varying degrees of severity throughout the 645 human societies that Murdock and his colleagues studied.[1]

Murdock found that the incest taboo has been practiced in every known society, thus bordering on the universal. This suggests to a functionalist that this taboo must be acknowledged if the community is to continue to exist in its present form of social organization. Other norms and practices (such as marital and death ceremonies) are found in all human communities. From the largest social units of analysis (let us say, the nation-state) to the smallest sociological unit of analysis, the dyad, there are rules that define the quality, degree, and extent of interaction between any two or more individuals.[2] In this chapter we are concerned specifically with the nature and social organization of the ethnic community.

Recently, Jessie Bernard has observed that a community has an all-encompassing, diffuse function in innumerable social settings.[3] What, if anything, she asks, do a nomadic tribe of Bedouins and a megalopolis like New York City, for example, have in common? The answer may lie with three salient characteristics that are usually agreed upon as a minimum definition of community — locale, common ties (blood and otherwise), and social interaction.[4]

Typically, sociologists employ the term community in two general senses. In the first, "the community" usually refers to settlements in which locale is a basic component. The community in this sense came with agriculture.[5] Among hunting peoples who had to go where the food was, or grazing peoples who had to follow their herds, locale did not have the meaning that it had later among agricultural peoples who settled in fixed locations. Bernard notes further that although the nomadic peoples were no less dependent on their land resources than were the agricultural peoples, the fact that they had to pull up stakes every season made their emotional attachments to any one geographical locale more tenuous.[6]

The second use of the term is "community," as distinguished from "the community," and emphasizes the common-ties and social-interaction components. In this sense community is viewed by some sociologists, including Robert Nisbet, as "the most fundamental and far-reaching of sociology's unit ideas."[7] It is characterized not so much by locale as by "a high degree of personal intimacy, emotional depth, moral commitment, social cohesion, and continuity in time."[8] Ferdinand Tönnies' usage of *Gemeinschaft* refers to community in the sense Nisbet describes.[9] It is older than the local community, and so is characteristic of nomadic tribes as well as of fixed agricultural settlements. It persists even today among gypsies who have no fixed geographical locale at all, and its essential forms remain, despite transformation, even in the most complex social setting, the metropolis. In both the locale and the *Gemeinschaft* conceptualization of community, we are dealing with some kind of unity, or co-unity, whatever the nature of the uniting bond.

This chapter addresses important implications of the function of community for a specific group. Bernard and others note that students of *gemeinschaftlich* community are also concerned with the effects of modern technology.[10] Related to this, we are interested in what happens to an ethnic community — in this case, the Japanese Americans — when its members advance socioeconomically. Does it mean the eventual disruption or disappearance of the community as it has historically been known? Or will the community remain intact among later generations as a place of refuge from assimilation into the larger American society? The results of our three generational study provide evidence toward an answer.

The Japanese American Community

In turning to an examination of the social fabric of the Japanese American community, it is useful to start with Miyamoto's 1939 study of the early immigration and community experiences of the Japanese in Seattle, Washington. If we can assume that the Seattle experience was similar to the Japanese experiences in Los Angeles, San Francisco, and other major Japanese communities, we can refer to Miyamoto's work as historical context for our present study.

Steiner has observed: "One of the striking characteristics of the Japanese in America is the thoroughness of their organization. . . . In their tendency to organize and in their ready response to group control, the Japanese have been equalled by few, if any, of the European groups."[11] The subject of Miyamoto's well-established work is what he terms the conspicuous characteristic of the Japanese communities — their pervasive solidarity.[12] This is a trait so characteristic of organized Japanese life that it justifies investigation in and of itself. The degree of Japanese Americans' assimiliation and the nature of their responses to discrimination are strongly influenced by internal community attitudes. The Japanese are community-builders or ghetto-seekers. According to Kiefer:

> Because they were a small group subjected to discrimination in housing and jobs and because they followed nonmigratory long

term occupations, the farmers, small businessmen, and service employees who made up a large proportion of the Japanese population from about 1910 on tended to settle in small urban ghettos and rural hamlets. These circumstances were ideal for the development of close-knit, highly cooperative, and tightly controlled ethnic communities.[13]

In order to understand fully the functioning of the Japanese community, we must conceptualize it as a group of interacting family units rather than as aggregates of discrete individuals. The latter characterization might more accurately describe Anglo-American community organization but would not apply to the Japanese. What would be strictly a private matter in an individualistic society tends to be a group enterprise in Japan.[14] The subordination of the individual to the group is so strong that actions that might be viewed as extreme self-sacrifice in other cultures are taken for granted as acts of group loyalty among the Japanese.[15]

In Japan the enlarged household is known as the *ie*, and this unit has been adopted and broadened in the United States to include the entire Japanese community. The *ie* concept as it was transplanted was so pervasive that it completely overshadowed the importance of the individual. The emphasis on group solidarity was so strong that the household member had virtually no existence apart from his role as a member of the *ie*.[16]

In the United States the entire Japanese community assumed the functions of the *ie* and became the reference group for the individual and the family. Thus the early families quickly became interdependent with the ethnic community at large and established a fundamental community solidarity as a framework for social experience and for meeting outside hostility.[17] Individuals were expected to behave in a manner that would reflect well on all Japanese. Lebra notes that an individual's pride and shame are shared by the group and in turn the individual assumes the pride and shame of the group as a whole.[18] The sense of obligation flows both ways: the individual feels a total commitment and loyalty to the group, and the group in turn is responsible for caring for each member. The community provides social opportunities for its members through Japanese language schools, cultural and recreational opportunities, and also serves effectively as the primary agency for social control.[19]

The Basis of Ethnic Solidarity

Although he acknowledges that the persistence of strong community organization among the Japanese is related to racial differences and prejudices, Miyamoto stresses the importance of examining the complex of antecedent cultural and historical factors behind this solidarity.[20] To a considerable extent the nature of the cultural background of the Japanese has slowed their absorption by the larger American society and thus gives functional significance to their community solidarity.

It is a reasonable assumption that an immigrant people such as the Japanese interprets its new environment with the values and attitudes of the old country, however open to change its members may be. In the case of the Japanese, these values are based upon the strong and very important ethical training system, brought with them from their native Japan, that is comprised of a set of social codes rigidly regulating social relationships, with a special reference to social rank.[21] The established ranking order is overwhelmingly important to the Japanese in terms of providing a secure social system in which everyone knows where he stands and what is expected of him when interacting with others. When two persons are unequal in status, the inferior person becomes dependent upon the higher ranking individual in a quasi-familial pattern.[22] They assume roles that resemble parent and child within any given situation. For example, within academia a professor will rarely challenge a professional paper by another member of his department who has equal or higher standing than he does (usually measured in terms of longevity). To do so would indicate disrespect and constitute a breach of etiquette.

Miyamoto emphasizes the importance and function of Japanese ethics:

> It is difficult to show the extent to which these ethical principles permeate the whole society, but to indicate briefly: the family, for instance, must eat, yet in this most mundane experience is interwoven a series of ethical traditions, such as that the head of the

family shall be served first, that food shall be offered to the dead at the family shrine, and so on. A visitor arrives, and about every exchange of greeting or remark, an ethical principle is distinctly involved. A young man and woman fall in love, but between the first-felt emotion and its consummation in marriage is a host of proprieties which must be observed. In other words, for every social act there is a socially proper as well as a socially improper way, and it is incumbent upon each member of this society to recognize what is the right way. In Japanese eyes society has no significance except as an interwoven whole of ethical meanings. These ethical meanings are *a priori* premises to all their social interpretations.

Understanding this fact, one may better realize the reasons for certain outstanding Japanese characteristics. Where social codes are defined in as much detail as in Japan, formalism and ceremonialism are functionally indispensable to the culture. Moreover, a vast system of etiquette, leading to an indirectness in communication and a strong awareness of social censors to individual action, are necessary. There is no need to enlarge upon the ramification of ideas that are related to their ethics, for, to put it briefly, that ramification encompasses their whole ideological system.[23]

Beyond this meaning of ethics, the code also entails the conception of duty, or *giri* (meaning, literally, "right reason"), a term which may be used interchangeably with "social obligation," or "social responsibility."[24] The extent of this social obligation or duty is almost endless. In Japan itself (at least until the end of World War II) the rules include duty to one's parents and family, to the neighborhood, the community, the nation, and—the supreme duty—to the emperor. From the concept of duty there follow other ethical requirements, including sacrifice, honor, loyalty, and courage. However, duty, or the conception of social responsibility, is the dynamic focus of the Japanese ethical system. Lebra has called this concept of obligation a "social preoccupation" among the Japanese.[25] Within the smallest family unit, interaction is based on *oyakoko*, or filial piety.[26] It represents a reciprocal obligation from parent to child and from child to parent, and can be observed in the simplest, day-to-day activity.

Again, the Japanese conception of the family is not limited as a

rule to the household.[27] Rather, there is a consistent tendency for
primary-group attitudes to reach beyond the limits of one's legal
kinsfolk and apply to the largest unit conceivable as a family. This
unit, in Japanese conception, takes in the entire nation, since
from an historical point of view the people consider themselves all
of one blood. It is important to note once more that the basis of
this social organization is the ethical system of collective obligations, and it is this that gives the Japanese family a degree of
solidarity difficult to conceive in the Western mind.

It is fairly easy to determine how in fact the Japanese establish
and enforce conforming behavior in their communities. DeVos,
for example, notes that central to the Japanese social organization
is the code of duties that defines the roles and obligations of the
members of that society.[28] The authority that enforces these
obligations is the Japanese belief in the superiority of the group
over the individual. Solidarity is maintained by forcing individuals to conform with the traditional group values, while
potential recalcitrants are kept in line by public opinion weighted
by the traditional ethical views. Fear of ridicule and ostracism
provide great motivation for conformist behavior, and from
childhood on the Japanese are controlled by what has been called
a shame-orientation.[29] As a result, the Japanese become extremely vulnerable to hurt feelings and develop acute sensitivity
to the feelings of others.[30] The ability to wound another person's
feelings thus becomes "an effective strategy for social sanction."[31]
From this system of interlaced ethical principles and social control, it becomes clear why in Japan it is the family and the community—not the individual—that are the basic social units. The
conception of the individual as secondary has profound
significance for the social organization and persistence of the
Japanese community.

According to Miyamoto, it is possible to refer to two distinct
aspects of the term "Japanese community."[32] The first is the to-
tality of Japanese living within the civic boundaries of a particular
community, the members of which feel a common bond with all
the rest of their nationality; the second meaning of community is
the central area within which all their major activities are conducted. In his study, Miyamoto considers his domain the second,
total community, for it is the solidarity of this aggregate that is

most significant. Adopting this perspective, we turn to an examination of the Japanese American immigration experience and
its implications for community organization and solidarity.

It was natural enough that the earliest contract laborers (who
arrived in 1885) remained, so far as possible, with others from
their same family, village, and prefecture. They "enjoyed the
company of their own *ken* folk, with whom they shared the same
dialect, the same birth and marriage customs, and often the same
Buddhist sect."[33] They formed *kenjinkais*, social organizations
based on prefectural origins, of which there were still nineteen
such groups listed in the 1964 Japanese telephone directory for
Los Angeles.[34]

Miyamoto notes that with the passing of years (particularly
after the 1907 signing of the Gentlemen's Agreement) the early so-
journing orientation ("getting-rich-quick" and returning home)
was set aside, since each year of life in the United States made ad-
justments easier and more congenial.[35] Consequently, the early
eagerness and urge to get back to Japan faded.

The roots of Japanese American ethnic and community
solidarity are often considered to be in the community's basic
orientation towards Japan. As Kitano observes:

> The Issei had been born into a social system that, although unlike
> the American system, peculiarly fitted them to adapt to the dif-
> ficulties they found here. From birth a Japanese was accustomed
> to put the interests of his family, village, ken, nation, and emperor
> ahead of his personal interests. His behavior was dictated by
> clearly defined rules and obligations. A system of collectivism and
> ethical interaction provided mutual assistance for group members
> and proved effective in protecting the individual from the cultural
> shocks of both a rapidly changing Japan and, later, of a new
> land.[36]

Although the early Issei had little power and few voluntary
alternatives within the larger American society, their cultural
background was congruent with middle-class American values
and kept them from becoming locked into the lower economic
stratum. One plausible reason for the lack of a "hard-core"
poverty population has been the ability of the ethnic community

to handle its own problems through its own organizations.[37] The early organizations were multifunctional, serving the needs of the Issei in religious, economic, and political areas.[38]

The Japanese Association was the most important Issei group. While most of its activities were directed toward such intra-community affairs as maintaining graveyards, providing transla-tors, and finding legal assistance, "the principal function of the Japanese Association, at least in the minds of its members, was protective."[39] As Petersen notes, part of its protective power was based in its relationship with the Japanese consulate, because the Issei were technically citizens of Japan.[40] Ethnic organizations "satisfied the emotional desires for personal association and enabled common action with organized means. . . . Although they served discrete ends, these organizations helped to restore a sense of stability and solidarity based on traditional patterns."[41] In general, the Issei groups played a conservative role in accul-turation. They were an important force in keeping the ethnic community "Japanese," but at the same time provided a voice whereby the Issei could deal with the Anglo community.[42] To that extent, the ethnic organizations helped to establish com-munication between the two cultures.

In spite of the strong family orientation among the Japanese, the relationship between the Issei and their children, the Nisei, was not apt to be close. The Nisei, who had no memories of Japan, felt not quite American and not quite Japanese and were truly comfortable only among other Nisei. They spoke English fluently and, while they maintained many basically Japanese at-titudes, they had acquired many American tastes and habits that their parents lacked.[43] Barriers of communication, while serving to avoid overt culture conflict, also prevented much direct paren-tal control.[44]

The Nisei broke away from the Japanese Associations of their parents and formed their own organization, the Japanese American Citizens' League (JACL), modeled after U.S. social and service organizations. This "enabled Nisei to set up their own goals, to operate from power positions, and to retain an identity."[45] Although the Issei would periodically attempt to exert control over their children's organizations, the Nisei in general successfully resisted these efforts.

From the very beginning, Nisei organizations leaned toward acculturation. The JACL led to increased communication with larger community organizations, and in general broadened the outlook of the Nisei. According to Kitano: "The general movement of Japanese community institutions was toward American models . . . [and] expectations changed for each ethnic generation, so that adherence to the ethnic community has had different meanings for Issei, Nisei, and Sansei."[46]

Miyamoto characterizes the development of the Seattle Japanese community as passing through various periods.[47] First was the Frontier Period, about the time of the 1907/1908 Gentlemen's Agreement, which limited immigration from Japan to the United States. Second was the Settling Period, after the time immigration was legally limited and members of the community were beginning to realize that they would never return to their homeland. This period also includes the coming of World War I. After the signing in 1921 of the Anti-Alien Land Law, which prohibited foreign-born Japanese from owning or leasing land, the Japanese were hit with still another legal blow, the passage of the Immigration Act of 1924. This act effectively prohibited further immigration of the Japanese to the United States. The period of 1924 to 1939 Miyamoto terms the "Second-Generation" period.

Thus the historical background of the Japanese was such that they could not leave the bosom of their community and cast off their ties completely. There was an earlier period when they might have broken away, but subsequent turbulent events drove them back and enhanced their solidarity. Had Japanese Americans discarded their heritage — their collectivistic tradition — in the thirty years or more of their residence in the United States, they undoubtedly would have accepted America more fully. But if they had, it is doubtful that their community solidarity would be as tenacious as it is today.

Having gained a grasp of the meaning of Japanese American community cohesiveness and solidarity and of the early cultural and historical factors that the Japanese encountered in their newly adopted land, we now turn to an examination of the extent to which succeeding generations have maintained community solidarity. With data from our three-generational, continental sample of Japanese Americans, we attempt to determine the extent of the Nisei and Sansei community immersion, affiliation, and interaction. The more salient the evidence we can bring to bear upon this question, the more likely it is that we shall be able to assess and to project the directions that the Japanese American community may take with regard to these characteristics, both within the forseeable future and when the next generation arrives (the *Yonsei*).

After a brief description of the study's design and the methods of data collection in the next chapter, we proceed to the question of the relation between the Nisei and Sansei socioeconomic mobility and the cohesiveness of their ethnic community.

Notes

1. G. P. Murdock, "World Ethnographic Sample."
2. Robert F. Bales, *Personality and Interpersonal Behavior*; and George C. Homans, *Social Behavior*.
3. Jessie Bernard, *The Sociology of Community*.
4. George A. Hillery, Jr., "Definitions of Community."
5. Bernard, *The Sociology of Community*, p. 3.
6. Ibid.
7. Robert Nisbet, *The Sociological Tradition*, p. 47.
8. Ibid.
9. Ferdinand Tönnies, *Community and Society*.
10. Bernard, *The Sociology of Community*.
11. Jesse F. Steiner, *The Japanese Invasion*, p. 130. Cited in S. Frank Miyamoto, "Social Solidarity among the Japanese in Seattle," p. 57.
12. Miyamoto, "Social Solidarity among the Japanese in Seattle," p. 57.
13. Christie Kiefer, *Changing Cultures, Changing Lives*, p. 97.
14. Takie Sugiyama Lebra, *Japanese Patterns of Behavior*, p. 25.
15. John W. Connor, *Tradition and Change in Three Generations of Japanese Americans*, p. 29.
16. Ibid.; and Kiefer, *Changing Cultures, Changing Lives*.
17. Harry H. L. Kitano, *Japanese Americans*, 2nd ed.
18. Lebra, *Japanese Patterns of Behavior*.
19. Harry H. L. Kitano, *Race Relations*.
20. Miyamoto, "Social Solidarity among the Japanese in Seattle," p. 58.

21. Ruth Benedict, *The Chrysanthemum and the Sword*; and Chie Nakane, *Japanese Society*.

22. Lebra, *Japanese Patterns of Behavior*, p. 50.

23. Miyamoto, "Social Solidarity among the Japanese in Seattle," pp. 59-60.

24. Kitano, *Japanese Americans*, 2nd ed., p. 44.

25. Lebra, *Japanese Patterns of Behavior*, p. 2.

26. Kitano, *Japanese Americans*, 2nd ed., p. 43.

27. Miyamoto, "Social Solidarity among the Japanese in Seattle," p. 60.

28. George A. DeVos, *Socialization for Achievement*.

29. Kiefer, *Changing Cultures, Changing Lives*.

30. Ibid.; and Lebra, *Japanese Patterns of Behavior*.

31. Lebra, *Japanese Patterns of Behavior*, p. 43.

32. Miyamoto, "Social Solidarity among the Japanese in Seattle," p. 63.

33. Bradford Smith, *Americans from Japan*, p. 57.

34. *Hokubei Mainichi Yearbook*. Cited in Kitano, *Japanese Americans*, 2nd ed., p. 66.

35. Miyamoto, "Social Solidarity among the Japanese in Seattle," p. 65.

36. Kitano, *Japanese Americans*, 2nd ed., pp. 53-54.

37. Ibid., p. 52.

38. William Petersen, *Japanese Americans*, p. 54.

39. Kitano, *Japanese Americans*, 2nd ed., p. 56.

40. Petersen, *Japanese Americans*, p. 57.

41. Oscar Handlin, "Historical Perspectives on the American Ethnic Group," pp. 223-225.

42. Kitano, *Japanese Americans*, 2nd ed., p. 56.

43. Kiefer, *Changing Cultures, Changing Lives*, pp. 97-98.

44. Kitano, *Japanese Americans*, 2nd ed., p. 50.

45. Ibid., pp. 67-68

46. Ibid., p. 55.

47. Miyamoto, "Social Solidarity among the Japanese in Seattle," pp. 65-66.

3
Methods of Study

This study is based upon three-generational data collected by the Japanese American Research Project (JARP) at UCLA. One of the early purposes of JARP was to sample and to interview surviving members of the first generation (the Issei) on the U.S. mainland, most of whom were becoming quite elderly. An attempt was made in 1963 to list every Issei immigrant still living in the United States, excluding Hawaii and Alaska. The lists were derived from membership lists of various Japanese American voluntary associations and churches, and totaled about 18,000 persons. Undoubtedly, these lists were incomplete, leaving out people who had failed to join an organization. The Japanese immigrant community, however, was one of the most highly organized of immigrant groups and the error is not nearly as great as it would be for some other immigrant nationalities.[1]

A sample was selected from these lists and interviewed in 1964-66. Less than 1 percent refused, producing a sample of 1,047 Issei. The Issei were asked for a complete listing of their children, the Nisei. This gave us a list of 3,817 Nisei, all of whom we attempted to contact either by personal interview, telephone interview, or mail questionnaire. A 60 percent response rate was achieved, yielding a Nisei sample of 2,304.[2]

Of the original 1,047 Issei, 141 did not have children or did not have children who responded to our questionnaire. Thus 906 Issei are parents of the people on whom the bulk of this study concentrates, the Nisei. An attempt was made to reach Issei families rather than individuals; when the man of the family was alive and well, he was interviewed rather than his wife. Thus, 64 percent of the Issei sample is male, including 75 widowers and 7 men who were divorced or separated. (The unmarried did not have children, of course, and are therefore being disregarded for the purposes of this study.) The large majority of the women (90 percent) were widows. Twenty-nine women (9 percent) had living husbands who, for various reasons, could not be interviewed, and 4 were divorced or separated.

Since an attempt was made to include all the offspring of each Issei in our Nisei sample, many of the Nisei are siblings. Table 3.1 shows this degree of relatedness for those families in which there were Nisei repondents. Each column represents a different actual family size. Thus there were 78 Issei with only one child, 138 with two children, 195 with three, and so on. The rows represent the number of Nisei who actually responded to the interview or questionnaire. Consider two-child Issei families, for example: for such families we have 67 cases in which only one of the siblings responded, and 71 cases in which both did (meaning that there are 142 Nisei who share a single brother or sister in the sample). For three-child Issei families, of which there are 195 in our Nisei sample, in 59 cases one out of the three responded, in 80 cases two of the three (meaning 160 Nisei), and in 56 cases all three answered (making 168 Nisei). Adding these up we find that 387 Nisei in our sample belong to three-child families.

The most important description of the interrelatedness of the sample (as opposed to the population from which it is drawn) appears in the last (summation) column. Here we find that 267 persons in the Nisei sample are not related to each other. There are 257 families with two sibling respondents, or 514 Nisei who have a single sibling in the sample. There are 181 three-sibling families, or 543 Nisei with two other siblings in the sample. Continuing in this manner, we see that finally there are 9 families with at least eight siblings in the sample, or at least 72 Nisei with eight or more brothers and sisters in our sample.

It will be noted that five families are missing from this table. Despite prodigious cleaning efforts at great expense there are still a few errors in the data and this represents one of them. In these five cases we have one more Nisei respondent than the Issei parent claimed was in his or her family. The number of Nisei thereby omitted from the table is nineteen.

In contacting the Nisei, special emphasis was placed on reaching the eldest son of the family, on the assumption that he would be the one primarily marked for a move up the socio-

Table 3.1

Response Rate by Family Size of Nisei Siblings

for All Families with At Least One Nisei Respondent

| Number of Nisei Responding | Number of Children Listed by Issei | | | | | | | | Σ |
	1	2	3	4	5	6	7	8+	
1	78	67	59	37	11	11	1	3	267
2		71	80	49	26	16	9	6	257
3			56	57	40	16	8	4	181
4				34	27	23	10	6	100
5					12	21	9	10	52
6						6	9	9	24
7							1	10	11
8+								9	9
Σ	78	138	195	177	116	93	47	57	901

The first column refers to the number of Nisei responding, regardless of the total number of siblings in a family. For example, Row 1, Column 3, reports that our sample contains 59 families which have three siblings, of which only one of those three siblings in the family responded to our survey. Thus the summation column reports the fact that our sample contains 267 Nisei who have no brothers and sisters in the sample.

economic ladder. The first wave of the Nisei phase of the study was conducted by face-to-face or (in a minority of cases) telephone interviews, and 95 percent of eldest sons were reached by these means. Most younger sons and daughters were reached with a mailed questionnaire. This emphasis on the eldest sons has affected the age-sex distribution in the sample, since there was obviously a higher response rate for those contacted more directly. Thus 52 percent of the Nisei sample is male, and there is a slightly higher proportion of older males than females (46 percent as compared with 42 percent born before 1925).

As with the Issei, the Nisei were asked to provide us with lists of their offspring. But in this case, since many of the Sansei were young children, we requested only those eighteen years of age or older. Thus, the sets of siblings are not usually complete families. This procedure gave us a list of 1,063 Sansei, of whom 802 or 76 percent responded to a mailed questionnaire.

The Sansei, like the Nisei, are related to each other, this time not only as siblings sharing common parents, but also as cousins sharing common grandparents. The families of siblings are shown in Table 3.2, which has the same structure as Table 3.1. Again, the columns represent the size of the family. Thus, seven Nisei listed seven children over seventeen years of age, fourteen listed six, thirty listed five, and so on. Within this potential pool of respondents, the rows once more show how many actually answered the questionnaire. In families with seven offspring, for example, in one case only one Sansei responded, in two cases two answered, in one case three answered, and in three cases four

Table 3.2

Response Rate by Family Size of Sansei Siblings

for All Families with At Least One Sansei Respondent

Number of Sansei Responding	Number of Children Listed by Nisei							Σ
	1	2	3	4	5	6	7	
1	41	84	81	40	10	5	1	262
2		58	53	35	7	6	2	161
3			13	16	7	3	1	40
4				10	4	0	3	17
5					2	0	0	2
6						0	0	0
7							0	0
Σ	41	142	147	101	30	14	7	482

See footnote on Table 3.1.

responded. This means that twenty of our Sansei respondents belong to families with seven siblings over seventeen years of age.

As in Table 3.1, the summation column shows the inter-relatedness of sample members. Thus, 262 Sansei do not have a brother or sister in the sample (even though only 41 do not have a sibling in real life who might have been included). There are 161 two-sibling families, or 322 Sansei with a sibling in the sample, and so on. Error has crept in at this stage too, and 20 Sansei are not included in this table.

As we have indicated, the Sansei in our sample not only stand a chance of having a brother or sister in the sample, they may also have cousins here. Table 3.3 depicts the nature of the sample in terms of this relationship. There are 348 cousin-sets in the Sansei sample, i.e., there are 348 Issei who have one or more grand-children in the sample. Of these, 143 Issei have only one grand-child who responded to our questionnaire, and these make up the limiting case of a "cousin-set."

Table 3.3

Size of Sansei Cousin-Sets, and the Number of

Nuclear Families of Which They Are Composed

Number of Nuclear Families in Cousin-set	Size of Cousin-Set								
	1	2	3	4	5	6	7	8+	Σ
1	143	73	13	6	1	0	0	0	236
2		21	30	18	11	2	2	0	84
3			0	9	5	4	1	3	22
4				0	0	0	0	3	3
5					1	0	0	0	1
6						0	0	2	2
Σ	143	94	43	33	18	6	3	8	348

For an explanation of this table's format, see footnote in Table 3.1.

The columns of Table 3.3 show the size of the cousin-sets. Each column lists the number of families of Sansei who share a common grandparent. Thus there are 94 Issei who have two grandchildren in the sample (or 94 two-person Sansei cousin-sets, or 188 Sansei who have a relative in the sample who share a common grandparent). There are 43 Issei who have three grandchildren in the sample (or 43 three-person cousin-sets, or 129 Sansei who have two other relatives in the sample who have a common grandparent).

But Sansei can share a grandparent and not necessarily be cousins. They may also be siblings. The rows in Table 3.3 show the number of nuclear families in each cousin-set. Consider four-person cousin-sets (of which there are thirty-three) as an illustration. For six of these, all four members belong to a single nuclear family, i.e., they share a grandparent, but they also share the same parents. They are not cousins. For eighteen families, there are two nuclear families, so that there are Sansei cousins in these families. The way they are distributed is not indicated here. It could be that each of the families has two Sansei, or that one has three and one has a single child. In any case, the four Sansei who make up each cousin-set are both siblings and cousins. Finally, nine of the four-person cousin-sets comprise three nuclear families. This means more cousin and fewer sibling relationships within the families.

Altogether, of the 348 three-generation families, 236 (or 68 percent) have only one nuclear family represented in the third generation. In other words, only about one-third of the families contain Sansei who are really cousins. Most of these (84 families or 75 percent of the remainder) are in two-nuclear family cousin-sets. Still, on the individual level, there are 446 Sansei who have at least one cousin in our sample.

There are a number of problems with our sample as far as representativeness is concerned. First, despite efforts to make the original Issei lists as complete as possible, these lists undoubtedly omitted some of those who were least tied to the Japanese American community. But even had the lists been complete, the endeavor itself had built-in biases. Only living Issei were sought, meaning that the sample consists only of families in which a member of the immigrant generation survived into the late 1960s. Our Nisei and Sansei samples omit the children and grandchildren of dead Issei.[3] In effect this means that our second and third generation samples are likely to be the progeny of Issei who came in the later phases of the migration to the United States.

Accurate comparisons with the 1960 census are impossible because foreign-born and Hawaiian-Japanese are included in the Japanese American figures. Separate figures are provided for Hawaii and for foreign-born, so that each can be subtracted from the totals. But they are not provided for Hawaiian foreign-born, so that we cannot assess the size of the overlap. Still, indications are that our Nisei and Sansei samples are overeducated. Among the Nisei, 42 percent did not pursue an education beyond high school, and for the Sansei the corresponding figure is 12 percent. In the 1960 census, even if we subtract the combined Hawaiian- and foreign-born (meaning that some people, those most likely to have little education, have been counted twice), 67 percent of Japanese in the United States have a high school education or less.

The fact that the sample is overeducated means that this study cannot describe the Japanese American community accurately. We do not have the correct parameters. What we are able to do is to analyze processes within the community, to explore the way certain aspects of social and economic life correlate with other aspects. Without a representative sample, such analysis must always remain tentative because the relationship might possibly shift among the undereducated.

Any attempt to get completely representative Nisei lists would have been incredibly more difficult than the already arduous task of obtaining Issei lists. Nisei are less likely to belong to Japanese American organizations, and thus, even this route would have been closed. We have managed to reach some of the nonmember children of Issei organization members. Although the sample is not technically perfect, we believe it is sound enough to enable us to draw some tentative conclusions about processes among the Japanese Americans.

Notes

1. Robert E. Park and Herbert A. Miller, *Old World Traits Transplanted*, p. 168.

2. We did interview by telephone some thirty-eight Nisei non-respondents in the Los Angeles area. They do not differ on key variables (e.g., education, occupation, income) from the respondents.

3. Using Los Angeles mortuary death lists, we did interview thirty-eight children of deceased Issei. They tend to be older than other Los Angeles Nisei respondents, but alike in other respects.

4

The Maintenance of the Japanese American Community: Nisei and Sansei Compared

Geographical Distribution of the Japanese American Population

As previously noted, the Japanese Americans are a tiny population of about one-half million (including Hawaii), thinly spread across the United States. Figure 4.1, based on U.S. Census data, shows that in 1900 only five states on the mainland (Montana, Idaho, Washington, Oregon, and California) had 1,000 or more Japanese American residents, and only California had 10,000 or more. By 1920 the Japanese Americans were still largely located in the Pacific Coast states, but they had branched out in large numbers into three additional states (Utah, Wyoming, and Colorado) and into one Eastern state (New York), each reporting from 1,000 to 10,000 Japanese American residents. Twenty years later, in 1940, the Japanese American population had diminished to less than 1,000 persons in the states of Montana and Wyoming, but had increased to over 10,000 in Washington, which thus became second only to California in the number of Japanese American residents within the continental United States.

The 1960 U.S. Census revealed dramatic shifts in the dispersion of Japanese Americans during the previous 20 years. The Census reports twenty-three states whose Japanese American residents number over 1,000. Additionally, Illinois joined ranks with Washington and California with over 10,000 Japanese Americans. With over 150,000 Japanese American residents, California became second only to Hawaii as a Japanese American center.

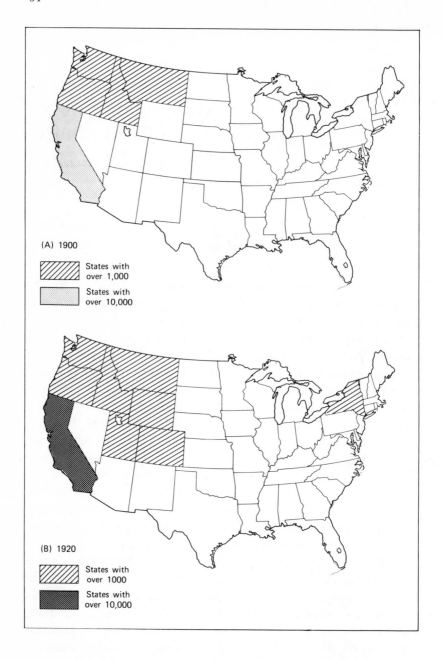

Figure 4.1. American Japanese population on the U.S. mainland. (Adapted with permission from Fellows, 1972:134-135; data from U.S. censuses)

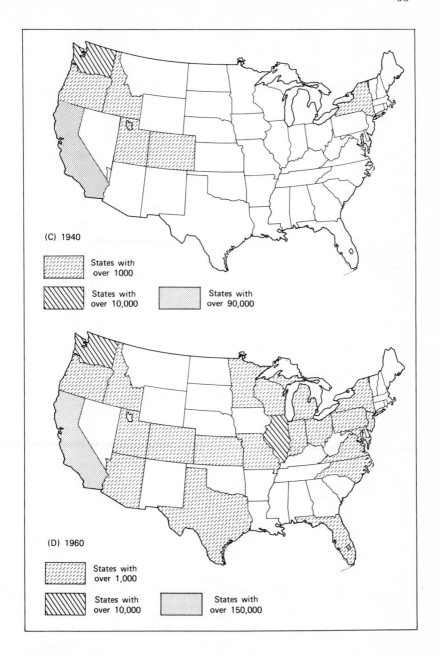

Figure 4.1 (continued)

The 1970 Census data (Figure 4.2) show that there were only five major centers of Japanese American population in the continental United States: Seattle, San Francisco, Los Angeles, Chicago, and New York. From these data it is clear that the Japanese are a thinly spread minority and that it may be difficult for them to maintain communal bonds across the nation. For further evidence, we turn to our three-generational survey data.

Broadly, our data indicate (Table 4.1) that 38 percent of respondents live in the metropolis of Los Angeles and, furthermore, that only 24 percent of the Nisei live away from the West Coast. As Figure 4.1 shows, even though twenty-three states have 1,000 or more Japanese Americans, there are still much higher concentrations in the five major centers of the United States.

With regard to the ethnic composition of the neighborhoods in which the Nisei presently reside, Table 4.1 reveals that only four

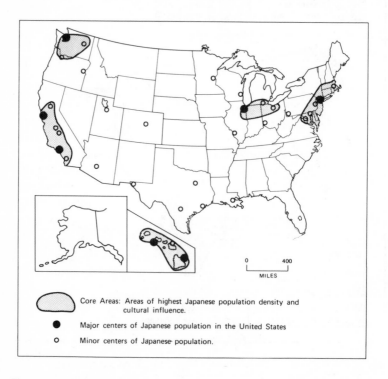

Core Areas: Areas of highest Japanese population density and cultural influence.

● Major centers of Japanese population in the United States

○ Minor centers of Japanese population.

Figure 4.2. Core areas of Japanese in the United States: 1970. (Adapted with permission from Fellows, 1972:136; data from U.S. censuses)

percent of the entire Nisei sample live in predominantly Japanese American neighborhoods, while a little over one-third live in mixed neighborhoods. Clearly then, the majority (58 percent) live in non-Japanese American neighborhoods. Meanwhile, the number living among Caucasians has increased to a majority — from 37 percent in 1915 to 58 percent in 1967.

Historically there has been a fairly dramatic change in neighborhood ethnicity for the Japanese Americans. Table 4.2 reports the changes in neighborhood ethnicity over a period of 52 years. We find that one-third (30 percent) of our 183 Nisei respondents living in 1915 reported that they resided in predominantly Japanese American neighborhoods. In fact, they were essentially evenly distributed, with approximately one-third in each of the categories: Japanese American neighborhoods, mixed neighborhoods, and mainly non-Japanese neighborhoods. Since 1915 the proportion of Nisei living in predominantly Japanese American neighborhoods has been steadily declining. Without exception it has decreased or remained the same for each of the periods from 1915 to 1967 for which our respondents reported.

This shift out of Japanese American ghettos and into Anglo neighborhoods would seem at first glance to suggest the demise of Japanese American ethnic communities as we have come to know them.[1] But we may well ask how the ethnic ties of these "non-ghetto" residents differ from those of the 42 percent who live in predominantly Japanese American and ethnically mixed neighborhoods. Does the quality and character of their ethnic community affiliation vary according to type of residence?

We find that fully 82 percent of our Nisei respondents live within the same city or county as one or more of their relatives (Table 4.3). Thus, a mere 17 percent are in this sense social isolates. Moreover, as many as 50 percent of the Nisei live within visiting distance of five or more relatives.

At a more intimate community level — the neighborhood — we find (Table 4.3) that a majority of Nisei (53 percent) live in the same neighborhood as one or more of their relatives and that almost one-third (30 percent) live among three or more kin. And at a still more intimate level, in the Japanese tradition of close-knit ties within the extended family, we find that almost one-

Table 4.1

Demographic Characteristics of the Nisei Sample

	Los Angeles	Pacific Coast[b]	Continental[c] U.S.	%	N
Current Residence[a]:	38%	39	24	101%	(2282)
Current Neighborhood Ethnicity:	Japanese American	Japanese American and Non-Japanese American	Non-Japanese American	%	N
	4%	38	58	100%	(2295)

[a]Current Residence based on 1967 Nisei interview reports.

[b]Pacific Coast, excluding Los Angeles.

[c]Remainder of Continental U.S., excluding Pacific Coast.

Table 4.2

Historical Changes in the Nisei Neighborhood Ethnicity

1915 - 1967

Year	Japanese American	Mixed	Non-Japanese American	%	N
1915	30%	33	37	100%	(183)
1920	22%	38	39	99%	(566)
1925	21%	41	39	101%	(1151)
1930	19%	43	38	100%	(1550)
1935	19%	44	38	101%	(1801)
1940	17%	45	38	100%	(1952)
1945	13%	36	51	100%	(1882)
1950	10%	44	47	101%	(2241)
1955	6%	44	50	100%	(2243)
1960	5%	43	52	100%	(2261)
1965	4%	41	55	100%	(2279)
1967	4%	38	58	100%	(2295)

quarter of the Nisei have one or more nonnuclear family relatives living in their household. Almost one in seven lives with two or more relatives.

While there are few comparative data regarding the differential presence of relatives within the same city by ethnic group, Lenski provides some comparative figures based upon interviews gathered through the Detroit area survey in 1952.[2] Lenski obtained information regarding those persons who had no relatives in the city of Detroit, except their immediate family living in the same dwelling unit. These are generally the people who have most completely severed their ties with the extended kin group. Lenski's findings revealed that 20 percent of the white Protestants fit into this category, compared with only 10 percent of the Catholics and Black Protestants, and 6 percent of the Jews.[3] This pattern of total separation from the kin group was especially pro-

Table 4.3

Nisei Ethnic Community Affiliation

	None	1-4	5-14	15+	%	N
Number of relatives[a] residing in same city or county as respondent:	17%	32	35	15	99%	(2259)
	None	1-2	3-6	7+		
Number of relatives[a] residing in respondent's neighborhood:	46%	23	20	10	99%	(2195)
	None	One	Two	Three+		
Number of relatives[a] residing in respondent's household:	76%	10	7	7	100%	(1173)

[a]Non-nuclear family relatives.

nounced among middle-class white Protestants. Fully 29 percent of this group reported no relatives living in the community other than those in the dwelling unit itself. This contrasted with only 9 percent of the middle-class Catholics, and none of the middle-class Jews. Among members of the working class, 20 percent of the Jews, 15 percent of the white Protestants, 10 percent of the Catholics, and 8 percent of the Black Protestants were "alone" in the community.

Sociological research on vertical mobility makes it abundantly clear that spatial mobility facilitates, or at least normally accompanies, vertical mobility.[4] If this is true, then people whose ties with kin bind them to their community of birth are necessarily at a disadvantage in the competition for advancement. This factor may well contribute to the different rates of mobility within our sample of Japanese Americans.

Nisei Community Interaction and Affiliation

Now that we have outlined the contours of the Japanese American population's distribution in the United States, it remains to ascertain whether or not opportunity for affiliation (e.g., the sheer presence of relatives in the same neighborhood, city, or county) actually results in interaction. That is, does the opportunity for communal participation translate itself in actual *association* with relatives and other ethnic brethren?

Table 4.4 shows that among Nisei who do have relatives in the same metropolitan area (city or county), 29 percent choose *not* to pay them regular visits. At the other end of the continuum, over one-third of the Nisei visit or are visited by relatives five or more times a month. These findings underscore the idea that the mere presence of relatives in the same metropolitan area does not automatically lead to the intensive visiting patterns one might expect. In the second generation, at least, the warmth of kinship ties has begun to abate. For many, opportunity for closeness does not necessarily make for close interaction. Table 4.4 reveals that almost 600 Nisei in the sample score as unaffiliated or perhaps even estranged from their kin and, in turn, perhaps from their community.

Lenski's study provides some comparative data for our

Table 4.4

Measures of Ethnic and Community Affiliation

				%	N
Number of monthly visits with relatives:	None 29%	One to Four 36	Five + 35	100%	(2064)
Number of affiliated organizations:	None 36%	One 23	Two 19	Three + 22	100%	(2236)
Number of affiliated Japanese American organizations:	None 57%	One 29	Two 14		100%	(2201)
Ethnicity of favorite affiliate organization:	Japanese American 45%		Non-Japanese American 55	100%	(1422)
Personally know an ethnic community leader:	Yes 51%		No 49	100%	(2092)
Two closest friends:	Both Japanese American 47%	One or Two Non-Japanese American 53		100%	(2239)

Japanese sample.[5] Lenski asked respondents how often they visited their relatives. The findings indicate that Jews were the most likely to visit relatives every week (75 percent), Catholics were the second most likely (56 percent), followed by White Protestants (49 percent) and Black Protestants (46 percent).

Using a cross-sectional national sample of male respondents, Klatzky found that ethnicity still had an impact on visiting patterns with fathers (after differences in living distance from fathers are taken into account). Klatzky found that of some thirteen ethnic groups, the Irish and Scandinavians have the most frequent contact with their parents.[6]

This finding contradicts the expectations that immigrants of the later waves of immigration (for example, Italians), would score highest in contact because of their strong family structure in the homeland. One tentative explanation is that the more assimilated, such as the Irish and Scandinavians, have had a longer time to develop a sturdy family structure in this country or did not originally meet with the extreme economic and social discrimination that undermined the stability of Southern European and particularly nonwhite families. Klatzky observes that the conditions of life and family structure in the country of ethnic origin appear to be less important than the length of time spent in the United States and/or the economic and social realities faced by various immigrant groups.

On another dimension of affiliation, that of organizational membership, of the 64 percent of our respondents who belong to one or more organizations (Table 4.4), only 43 percent belong to a Japanese American organization. As a more discriminating indicator of those who belong to an organization, over one-half (55 percent) devote the most time to a non-Japanese organization.

Similarly, Lopata's study of Polish-American organizational affiliation reveals the same general pattern. Her findings indicate that 50 percent of the first generation, 42 percent of the second, and only 30 percent of the third belong to a Polish organization. Moreover, she indicates that the third generation is much less active in voluntary organizations, either Polish-American or purely American, than are prior generations. She cautions, however, that these differences between the second and third generations may be due to age differences. It is interesting that the less educated older generation is very active in voluntary associations.[7]

On yet another dimension of community affiliation, personal friendship with an ethnic community leader, Table 4.4 shows that about one-half of the Nisei do know such a leader, while the other half knows one by reputation only or not at all.

Finally, with regard to one of the most telling indicators of community affiliation available to us, our data reveal that over one-half (53 percent) of all Nisei respondents claim that one or both of their two closest friends are of non-Japanese background. Comparative data regarding the ethnicity of a respondent's closest friends are quite limited. Joan Moore reported upon data collected from samples of Mexican Americans in Albuquerque, Los Angeles, and San Antonio. The ethnicity of present friends ranged from a high of 55 percent (of the San Antonio sample) having all Mexican Americans as their present friends, to a low of 22 percent and 27 percent (for Albuquerque and Los Angeles, respectively). Unfortunately, our data are not precisely comparable with Moore's data. We asked our Nisei and Sansei respondents the ethnicity of their two closest friends, *excluding relatives*. Our respondents report that 47 percent of the Nisei have ethnic Japanese as their two closest friends; whereas for the Sansei just over one-quarter (26 percent) report as many intraethnic friendships.[8]

In a second study that examines the issue, Cohen used two samples (a New York and a national sample) of several ethnic groups. The national sample was divided into three categories: (1) old migration Protestants (British, Germans, Irish, Dutch, Norwegians, Scots, and Swedes), (2) old migration Catholics (British, Germans, and Irish), and (3) new migration Catholics (Italians, Poles, and Spanish, including Puerto Ricans and Mexicans). Cohen's findings regarding the differential rates of intraethnic friendship varied considerably. The rates of intraethnic friendship for old migration Protestants and Catholics averaged only 16 percent for each group, whereas over one-third (38 percent) of the new migration Catholics claimed intraethnic friendships. For the New York sample, which was predominantly first and second generation, intraethnic friendships varied as follows: Irish Catholics, 63 percent; Puerto Rican Catholics, 65 percent; Jews, 72 percent; and American Blacks, 78 percent. Cohen found low rates of intraethnic marriage for the old migration Protestants and Catholics, but high rates for new migration Catholics and for his New York sample.[9] Cohen concluded that if exogamy is considered a reasonably valid indicator of assimilation, then virtually all old migration groups are substantially assimilated.[10] Hence, the issue of determining whether social class is associated with ethnic assimilation — for these groups — becomes a moot point.

How can an ethnic community, such as that of the Japanese Americans, maintain its level of communal interaction and affiliation when evidence in terms of neighborhood ethnicity, visiting patterns, organizational membership, and friendship patterns suggest a weakening of the ethnic ties? An important group to consider is the 600 Nisei who do not appear to be ethnically affiliated. Are they outcasts, or willing converts to another way of life? Is their action purposeful or accidental? The above data suggest that simple opportunity for interaction is not enough to make for community affiliation and interaction. We turn now to a consideration of these apparent social isolates.

Visiting Patterns and Socioeconomic Status

Table 4.5 presents data on visiting patterns in terms of four major independent variables: age, sex, occupation, and education.

Age and Visiting Patterns. We expect that age would be positively related to visiting patterns. The younger Nisei are at the same time both more highly educated and occupationally more upwardly mobile than their older peers. We therefore reasoned that they would be moving toward greater integration with the larger American society, and therefore would be less immersed in their ethnic communities as compared with older, less educated peers. Table 4.5 partially supports our expectation. The older Nisei are somewhat more likely to visit their relatives than are their younger counterparts. Almost one-half (47 percent) of the oldest Nisei, 54 years and older, visit one to four times per month, while one-third (33 percent) of the younger Nisei, 33 and younger, visit at this rate.

Among those who visit relatives five or more times per month, we find essentially no linear relationship with age. In fact, one-third (36 percent) of the youngest Nisei visit their relatives five or more times per month, and only 29 percent of the oldest Nisei visit that often. But still our general findings suggest that the youngest Nisei are somewhat less immersed in their ethnic community. Similarly, in a study of a national sample of male respondents, Klatzky reports that the youngest and oldest respondents have the most frequent contact with relatives.[11]

Sex and Visiting Patterns. We reasoned that female Nisei would be the more frequent visitors with relatives by far, since we found with other indicators of Japanese culture that the women tend to be important culture carriers. They more often retain the traditional Buddhist affiliation and are able to speak and to read Japanese more fluently than their male counterparts. We thus suspected that on this indicator, too, they would more often seek to maintain family and community affiliation through visiting their relatives. But Table 4.5 reveals that there are no essential differences between male and female visiting patterns. Similar findings were reported by Adams in his study of some 800 Greensboro, North Carolina, respondents. Adams reports that there were essentially no sex differences in respondents visiting their parents.[12]

Occupation and Visiting Patterns. Third, we reasoned that visiting patterns would be related to occupation, since some occupations (such as farming, gardening, and small business proprietorships that serve the Japanese American community) are likely to be affiliated with the ethnic economy.[13] The results of our cross-tabulation of male Nisei visiting patterns by occupation support our hypothesis.[14] We find that Nisei professionals are the least likely to visit their relatives frequently. Only one in four of Nisei professionals visit five or more times a month, whereas at the other end of the continuum farmers are the most frequent visitors of relatives. More than four in ten visit that often. Table 4.5 also shows that white-collar Nisei are more likely than blue-collar Nisei to visit frequently. This relationship is consistent with data reported by Klatzky in her study of a national sample of male respondents.[15] Although the theoretical literature suggests that blue-collar workers visit their parents and other relatives more often, our findings as well as Klatzky's reveal a small, yet con-

Table 4.5

Visiting Patterns as a Measure of Community Affiliation by Nisei Socioeconomic Status

About how many times in the past month have you visited with or been visited by relatives living in the same neighborhood or metropolitan area or county as you?

	None	1 to 4	5 or more	%	N	Gamma
Age						(+.04)
< 33 years	31%	33	36	100%	(382)	
34 to 43 years	31%	35	34	100%	(756)	
44 to 53 years	26%	38	36	100%	(824)	
54 years or older	24%	47	29	100%	(96)	
Sex						(+.01)
Male	28%	36	34	100%	(1084)	
Female	29%	34	36	99%	(980)	
Occupation (Males only)						(+.19)
Professional	39%	37	24	100%	(359)	
Proprietor	22%	37	41	100%	(195)	
Clerical	24%	35	40	99%	(124)	
Blue Collar	21%	45	35	101%	(139)	
Service	21%	46	33	100%	(100)	
Farmer	21%	36	43	100%	(132)	
Education						(-.18)
≤ High School (0 to 12 years)	23%	40	37	100%	(864)	
Some College (13 to 15 years)	25%	34	41	100%	(635)	
College Graduate (16 years)	37%	36	26	99%	(281)	
Postgraduate (over 17 years)	45%	31	24	100%	(280)	

sistently more frequent, visiting pattern for white-collar respondents than their blue-collar peers.[16]

In a second study regarding this issue, Bruce found that the occupationally mobile visited proportionally less often with siblings.[17] Moreover, the relationship continued to hold while controlling present socioeconomic level and occupational position.

As a further explanation of this phenomenon, Lenski has observed that one of the best indicators of the importance attached to the family and kin group by modern Americans is their willingness, or unwillingness, to leave their native community and migrate elsewhere.[18] Migration of this type generally involves a physical separation of the individual from those relatives with whom he has the closest ties. He may take some of these relatives with him, but rarely all of them. A person usually migrates in response to the lure of economic or vocational opportunities; hence, we may regard migration as an indicator of the importance he attaches to the kin group when its ties compete directly with the prospect of more money or a better job. Similarly, this thesis is echoed by Schneider and Homans who note that upwardly mobile persons keep only shallow ties with members of their kindred, if they keep them at all.[19]

In yet another study of correlates of mobility, Strodtbeck's study of Italian Catholic and Jewish families in New Haven, Connecticut, reveals that the greater economic success of the Jews was, in part, a function of their greater willingness to leave kith and kin.[20] Jewish boys were much more likely than Italian boys to disagree with the statement that "nothing in life is worth the sacrifice of moving away from your parents." While considerable caution must be exercised in interpreting these findings, since obviously Italian Catholics are not typical of all Catholics, nevertheless the similarity between these two sets of findings suggests the possibility of a more general pattern.

In a third study of the impact of occupational status on visiting patterns, Adams found that blue-collar kin networks are characterized by less residential dispersion, the result being that more frequent blue-collar interaction with various kin occurs.[21] In short, Adams concludes that in comparing the upwardly mobile with the stable blue collar in terms of interaction frequency with kin, he concurs with the thesis echoed by Schneider and Homans.[22] That is, the mobile have weaker or shallower kin ties.

Education and Visiting Patterns. Finally, we related visiting patterns to Nisei educational levels. We predicted that the attainment of higher education by placing one on the heterogeneous college campus for four or more years must dramatically change the texture of one's relationships with peers and family. The college years can be a period of resocialization during which new values and attitudes may be formed and old ones unlearned — to say nothing of changes in the patterning of social relationships.

Table 4.5 clearly supports our hypothesis. We find that Nisei with postgraduate training are the least likely to visit relatives frequently. About one in four do so as compared with over one in three of their high school educated peers. At the other end of the visiting continuum, almost one-half of postgraduate Nisei are nonvisitors as compared to only one-fourth of the high school educated.

Ethnicity of Favorite Organization and Socioeconomic Status

On a second dimension of community affiliation and involvement, we asked the Nisei respondents about the ethnic makeup of the organization to which they devote the bulk of their leisure time. We examined the relationship between our independent variables (age, sex, occupation, and education) and ethnicity of favorite organization.

Age and Ethnicity of Favorite Organization. We reasoned that, should the Nisei spend more of their leisure time in a non-Japanese American membership organization, this would indicate a move away from the ethnic community and toward structural assimilation. The younger Nisei, we predicted, would be more likely than their elders to favor a non-Japanese American organization. Table 4.6 reports that the youngest Nisei are much more likely than their elders to favor a nonethnic organization. Given that the younger Nisei tend to have higher educational and occupational status than the older, it follows that they would be more concerned with professional groups rather than local ethnic associations, and consequently they would be more likely to choose as their favorite organization one related to their professional calling.

Table 4.6

Ethnicity of Favorite Organization as a Measure of
Community Affiliation by Nisei Socioeconomic Status

	Japanese American	Non-Japanese American	%	N	Gamma
Age					(-.18)
≤ 33 years	37%	63	100%	(171)	
34 to 43 years	41%	59	100%	(547)	
44 to 53 years	48%	52	100%	(626)	
53 years or older	61%	39	100%	(76)	
Sex					(+.19)
Male	49%	51	100%	(815)	
Female	39%	61	100%	(607)	
Occupation (males only)					(-.37)
Professional	30%	70	100%	(278)	
Proprietor	52%	48	100%	(146)	
Clerical	56%	44	100%	(082)	
Blue Collar	57%	43	100%	(086)	
Service	81%	19	100%	(083)	
Farmer	57%	43	100%	(122)	
Education					(±.45)
≤ High School (0 to 12 years)	63%	37	100%	(579)	
Some College (13 to 15 years)	46%	54	100%	(407)	
College Graduate (16 years)	37%	63	100%	(214)	
Postgraduate (over 17 years)	21%	79	100%	(220)	

Sex and Ethnicity of Favorite Organization. Table 4.6 reports the relationship between sex and the ethnic makeup of the Nisei's favorite and regularly attended organization. We had expected again that females, given their traditionally closer link to their ethnic community, would disproportionately choose a Japanese American association. The findings, however, reveal that the reverse is the case; females are less likely than males to choose a Japanese American organization as their favorite. Briefly, this finding may be accounted for partly by the women's membership in organizations related to their children, such as the Parent-Teacher's Association (PTA).

Occupation and Ethnicity of Favorite Organization. Table 4.6 shows that only one-third (30 percent) of the Nisei professionals choose a Japanese American organization as their favorite, as against 80 percent of the service workers. As noted earlier, professional occupational status brings with it other cross pressures and commitments that intervene and may take priority over local, family, and ethnic concerns.

Education and Ethnicity of Favorite Organization. Although we found that occupation and organizational ethnicity have a moderate (negative) association (gamma = -.37), we find that education is more strongly and negatively related to organizational affiliation.[23] Nisei with only a high school education are three times more likely (63 percent) to choose a Japanese American organization as their favorite than those Nisei who have done postgraduate college work (21 percent).

The results relating to education and occupation are very similar, since the two variables are themselves so highly related. But the two factors need not go hand in hand. The findings for occupation show that 30 percent of the professionals choose a Japanese American organization as their favorite compared with 21 percent of those with a postgraduate education. This nine percent difference is probably a result of education serving as a more precise measure of social status than does occupation.

Friends' Ethnicity and Nisei Socioeconomic Status

Next we turn to a measure of more intimate social and community interaction — the ethnicity of the two persons described by the respondent as closest friends. We asked the Nisei to report the ethnicity of their two closest friends, excluding their relatives. These data should provide a sensitive indicator of the degree to which the Japanese American is tied to the ethnic community. Table 4.7 reports the relationships between the four independent variables (age, sex, occupation, and education) and the ethnicity of the two closest friends.

Age and Ethnicity of Two Closest Friends. Almost six in ten of the youngest Nisei respondents named Caucasians as one or both of their closest friends, as against four in ten for the older Nisei (54 years or over). Again, we believe that both education and occupation affect this relationship. The younger Nisei tend to have higher educational and occupational status, both of which are strongly related to disaffiliation from the community and, in turn, assimilation into the larger American society.

Sex and Ethnicity of Two Closest Friends. Since Nisei women are typically the bearers of certain traditional features of the culture, it was thought that they, more than their male counterparts, would have Japanese Americans as their best friends. Traditionally, they have been more homebound than the men and perhaps less in contact with non-Japanese.

The results in Table 4.7 reveal that essentially there is *no* difference between the male and female Nisei in their choice of closest friends. In fact, the females are slightly more likely to have a non-Japanese as one or both of their closest friends. This may be the result of residential patterns. The Nisei women in Caucasian neighborhoods may do more visiting and form more friendships than the Nisei men.

Connor's study of some 200 Nisei in Sacramento, California, likewise reports essentially no difference by sex in the selection of closest friends.[24] Our data reveal a 6 percent difference, whereas Connor reports a difference of only 2 percent between male and female respondents.

Occupation and Ethnicity of Two Closest Friends. We expected to encounter differences between Nisei professionals and blue-collar workers in their choice of friends, and the data in Table 4.7 support the conjecture. Professional Nisei are more than twice as likely as service workers to have non-Japanese friends. Six in every ten of the male Nisei professionals, against only three in ten of the service workers, have Caucasian friends.

Table 4.7

Ethnicity of Two Closest Friends as a Measure of Community Affiliation by Nisei Demographic Characteristics

	One or both Non-Japanese	Japanese American	%	N	Gamma
Age					(+.13)
≤ 33 years	58%	42	100%	(413)	
34 to 43 years	53%	47	100%	(835)	
44 to 53 years	51%	49	100%	(883)	
54 years or older	43%	57	100%	(100)	
Sex					(-.08)
Male	50%	50	100%	(1170)	
Female	56%	44	100%	(1068)	
Occupation (males only)					(+.29)
Professional	64%	36	100%	(387)	
Proprietor	47%	53	100%	(203)	
Clerical	47%	53	100%	(137)	
Blue Collar	45%	55	100%	(143)	
Service	31%	69	100%	(109)	
Farmer	39%	61	100%	(153)	
Education					(+.28)
High School (0 to 12 years)	45%	55	100%	(945)	
Some College (13 to 15 years)	53%	47	100%	(678)	
College Graduate (16 years)	56%	44	100%	(312)	
Postgraduate (over 17 years)	73%	27	100%	(299)	

Again, when a Nisei is in the professional ranks he is in greater contact with the surrounding Anglo society—first through the experience of Anglo-dominant higher education and, second, through the predominantly Anglo-populated professions, with the concomitant push and pull of professional demands and associations.

Education and Ethnicity of Two Closest Friends. We find that education is positively related to non-Japanese friendship choices: the higher the educational attainment, the more likely Nisei respondents are to have one or more Anglo friends. Whereas twice as many professionals as service workers have one or more Caucasian friends, the difference between the postgraduate educated and the high school educated is not as large (73 percent and 45 percent, respectively).

Spouse Ethnicity and Socioeconomic Status

Social scientists generally agree that one of the most telling indicators of the degree of assimilation of one ethnic group into another is the extent of outmarriage from the immigrant to host society.[25] Gordon, for example, notes that intermarriage is a natural stage in the assimilation of a minority group to the host society:

> If children of different ethnic backgrounds belong to the same play group, later the same adolescent cliques, and at college the same fraternities and sororities; if the parents belong to the same country club and invite each other to their homes for dinner; it is completely unrealistic not to expect these children, now grown, to love and marry each other, blithely oblivious to previous ethnic extraction.[26]

Our interest is to determine the extent to which outmarriage provides a good indicator of the disruption of social ties and the severing of affiliation from the Japanese American community. The Japanese Americans have had a long tradition of discouraging outmarriage. This has perhaps been in part a strategy of survival, given their small numbers, and in part, related to Japanese feelings of propriety. Although the outmarriage rate for the immigrant Issei was less than 1 percent, it increased among their Nisei children to approximately 10 percent. In turn, as we shall see below, it is increasing even more rapidly among the grandchildren, the Sansei — some 40 percent have outmarried. If the number of outmarriages should escalate rapidly, this tiny minority would soon disappear as a distinct ethnic group.

At this point, in order to have a benchmark, it is useful to examine other rates of ethnic intermarriage. While our comparative intermarriage data do not provide overall rates of intermarriage, they do provide percentage rates by sex of those individuals who marry outside their ethnic group. Census Bureau data indicate that white females outmarry at the rate of .3 percent, and white males choose other than a white spouse .4 percent of the time. American Indians have the highest rate of intermarriage: 39 percent of the women outmarry, and 35.8 percent of the men marry out of their ethnic group. For Blacks the percentage of intermarriage is 0.7 for women and 1.5 for men; for Chinese it is 12.2 and 13.5; Filipinos, 27.2 and 33.5; Mexicans, 16.7 and 16.1; and Puerto Ricans, 18.2 and 19.4. Of particular interest is the rate for Japanese. We find that almost one in three (33.2 percent) Japanese women marry non-Japanese, whereas only slightly more than one in ten (11.4 percent) Japanese men outmarry.[27] Clearly, if we find that socioeconomic status is positively related to outmarriage, the substantial educational and occupational gains the Nisei and the Sansei are making would lead us to predict an accelerating rate of outmarriage among Japanese Americans in the future. Table 4.8 sheds some light on this subject.

Age and Spouse Ethnicity. In our sample, age is inversely related to outmarriage (gamma = -.39). That is, the younger the Nisei, the more likely he or she is to marry a non-Japanese American. Over one in five of our youngest Nisei (thirty-three years of age and younger) have outmarried, as opposed to one in twenty of their peers fifty-four years of age or older. This finding is consistent with the view that the younger Nisei tend to be less traditional than the older Nisei. Owing to the younger Nisei's relatively high socioeconomic status, they are more often thrust into the larger Anglo society, not only for career advancement but also for mate selection.

Sex and Spouse Ethnicity. Assuming that Nisei women generally tend to be more traditional in terms of religion, language, and

Table 4.8

Spouse Ethnicity as a Measure of Affiliation by Nisei Socioeconomic Status

	Japanese American	Non-Japanese American	%	N	Gamma
Age					(−.39)
≤ 33 years	78%	22	100%	(226)	
34 to 43 years	90%	10	100%	(704)	
44 to 53 years	94%	6	100%	(760)	
54 years and older	94%	6	100%	(71)	
Sex					(−.07)
Male	89%	11	100%	(902)	
Female	91%	9	100%	(862)	
Occupation (males only)					(+.28)
Professional	84%	16	100%	(289)	
Proprietor	94%	6	100%	(182)	
Clerical	91%	9	100%	(95)	
Blue Collar	90%	10	100%	(111)	
Service	92%	8	100%	(89)	
Farmer	95%	5	100%	(131)	
Education					(+.37)
≤ High School (0 to 12 years)	94%	6	100%	(797)	
Some College (13 to 15 years)	91%	9	100%	(511)	
College Graduate (16 years)	87%	13	100%	(234)	
Postgraduate (over 17 years)	78%	22	100%	(221)	

Japanese culture than the men, outmarriage would be expected to be less frequent for the women. As in other cases contingent upon this view of Nisei women, however, the findings do not support the expectation. Table 4.8 reveals essentially no relationship between respondents' sex and outmarriage. Regardless of respondents' sex, approximately one in ten Nisei have outmarried.

Unlike our findings, the Census data indicate that the difference in outmarriage by sex is substantial: 33.2 percent of the women outmarry, whereas only 11.4 percent of Japanese men outmarry.[28] It is difficult to reconcile these substantial differences. Two possible explanations are relevant. First, the Census intermarriage data do not control for respondent's generation. Thus while the outmarriage rate for our Nisei sample is only 10 percent, it climbs to 40 percent of the Sansei respondents. Second, and probably most important, the Census data include Hawaii. Our sample purposely excludes Hawaiian Japanese from the study. Therefore the higher rates of interethnic marriages in Hawaii may, in part, explain the substantially higher outmarriage rates reported by the Census Bureau.[29]

Occupation and Spouse Ethnicity. There is a low association between occupational status and outmarriage. We encounter an irregular relationship between these two variables. Although the Nisei professionals have the highest outmarriage rate (one in six) and the farmers have the lowest (one in twenty), little else is consistent. The findings at the extremes are clearly related to mate-selection opportunity, education, and style of living. The daily experiences of the Nisei professional would more often bring him or her into contact with non-Japanese, and the reverse is true of the Nisei farmer (setting aside for the moment the impact of education on the availability and choice of mate).

Education and Spouse Ethnicity. We expected education to be the most reliable predictor of rate of outmarriage. Table 4.8 reveals a moderate, positive association between these two variables (gamma = + .37). The higher the Nisei's education, the greater the likelihood that the marriage will be exogamous. Whereas only one in twenty Nisei at the lowest rungs of the educational ladder has outmarried, one in every five Nisei at the highest educational rung has chosen a non-Japanese mate. As discussed above, this may be largely a result of attendance at predominantly white col-

lege campuses for five or more years, with the concomitant inter-
nalization of new values and attitudes during that period of
resocialization.

We have seen that two of our central independent variables, occupation and education, have a substantial impact upon ethnic
community affiliation and interaction. The highly educated professional Nisei, as compared with their blue-collar peers, have
lessened their ties with their ethnic communities to the greatest
extent, and in some cases have cut off interaction altogether and
have become largely assimilated. They are much less likely to visit
their relatives, choose a Japanese American organization as their
favorite, name a Japanese American as their closest friend, and
marry within their own ethnic group.

This is hardly to predict the total dissolution of the Japanese
American community, but these findings do require examination.
The Sansei are advancing socioeconomically at an even faster
pace than their Nisei parents. What of the Sansei? Will they
undergo a cultural renaissance, as discussed by some writers?[30]
Or will their socioeconomic mobility make for a weakening of
primary kinship ties and still greater communal dispersion?

A Comparative Portrait of the Issei, Nisei, and Sansei

Almost eight out of ten of both the Nisei and Sansei live on the
West Coast and one in every three lives in Los Angeles (Table
4.9). Even though most of our Sansei sample have lived within
proximity of others of their ethnic group, only 32 percent report
that their parents wanted them to limit their friendships to other
Japanese Americans while growing up. And a bare 9 percent
report that they would want their own children or future children,
the Yonsei, so to sequester themselves. Our results indicate clearly the desire of both Nisei and Sansei to navigate in the larger
Caucasian society.

According to Kiefer, the Nisei are quick to emphasize their
Americanness both among themselves and when dealing with the
larger society.[31] One overt expression of this emphasis is their ob-
jection to the hyphen in Japanese-American, because they feel it
subordinates their American identity to their Japanese identity.
Kiefer also affirms that the Sansei grew up in a family and com-

Nisei and Sansei Differential Community Affiliation

Nisei

Region	Los Angeles	Pacific Coast	Other Region	%	N
	38%	39	23	100%	(2282)

Relatives in Metropolitan Area	None	1 to 4	5 to 14	15+	%	N
	17%	32	35	15	99%	(2259)

Relatives in Neighborhood	None	1 to 6	7+	%	N
	46%	43	10	99%	(2195)

Neighborhood Ethnicity	Both Japanese and Non-Japanese	Non-Japanese	%	N
	42%	58	100%	(2295)

Monthly Visits With Relatives	None	1 to 4	5+	%	N
	29%	36	35	100%	(2064)

Reads Japanese American Newspaper	Regularly	Occasionally	Never	%	N
	35%	29	36	100%	(2300)

Sansei

Region	Los Angeles	Pacific Coast	Other Region	%	N
	35%	44	22	100%	(784)

Relatives in Metropolitan Area	None	1 to 4	5 to 14	15+	%	N
	17%	15	32	36	100%	(778)

Relatives in Neighborhood	None	1 to 6	7+	%	N
	53%	33	14	100%	(786)

Neighborhood Ethnicity	Both Japanese and Non-Japanese	Non-Japanese	%	N
	33%	67	100%	(801)

Monthly Visits With Relatives	None	1 to 4	5+	%	N
	23%	42	35	100%	(695)

Reads Japanese American Newspaper	Regularly	Occasionally	Never	%	N
	14%	32	54	100%	(802)

Table 4.9 (Continued)

Nisei

Present or Preferred Occupation

Profes-sional	Pro-prietor	Cleri-cal	Blue Collar	Service Worker	Farm-er	%	N
32%	19	14	12	10	13	100%	(2211)

(Continued)

Education

High School	Some College	College Grad-uate	Post-grad-uate	%	N
43%	30	14	13	100%	(2300)

Ethnicity of Two Closest Friends

One or Both Non-Japanese	Both Japanese	%	N
53%	47	100%	(2239)

Religion

Buddhist	Christian	None	%	N
37%	54	9	100%	(2229)

Ethnicity of Favorite Organization

Japanese Membership	Non-Japanese Membership	%	N
45%	55	100%	(1422)

Spouse Ethnicity

Japanese	Non-Japanese	%	N
90%	10	100%	(1765)

Sansei

Present or Preferred Occupation

Profes-sional	Pro-prietor	Cleri-cal	Blue Collar	Service Worker	Farm-er	%	N
73%	7	11	4%	4	1	100%	(676)

Education

High School	Some College	College Grad-uate	Post-grad-uate	%	N
12%	64	12	12	100%	(801)

Ethnicity of Two Closest Friends

One or Both Non-Japanese	Both Japanese	%	N
74%	26	100%	(795)

Religion

Buddhist	Christian	None	%	N
24%	56	20	100%	(786)

Ethnicity of Favorite Organization

Japanese Membership	Non-Japanese Membership	%	N
31%	69	100%	(218)

Spouse Ethnicity

Japanese	Non-Japanese	%	N
60%	40	100%	(238)

munity where the value of assimilation into American culture was not seriously questioned, where group identity carried a strong mainstream-American flavor.[32]

Further, the respondents were asked about the ethnicity of their two closest friends. An astounding three in four of the Sansei report that at least one of their closest friends is non-Japanese (Table 4.9). Neither were the Nisei divorced from intimate bonds with non-Japanese. Of course, as we have noted, over half of the Nisei respondents report interethnic friendships. Even so, we see that although the Sansei resemble the Nisei, they tend to be even more absorbed in the nonethnic society. When queried, 70 percent of the Sansei respondents were still single. We shall turn later to the matter of ethnicity in choice of a mate.

Although the large majority of the Sansei have non-Japanese friends, this does not mean that they feel themselves completely at home in the larger context. As many as 23 percent say that as Japanese Americans they are in some ways hindered in their social progress. But 66 percent remark that ethnic and racial identification appreciably hindered their parents' lives, thus indicating that most Sansei feel some progress has been made in the struggle against discrimination.

Among our Sansei sample only 38 percent have begun their own independent lives — that is, they have married or are no longer living under the parental roof and usually have independent means (although some of the married are still students). Thus six in ten of the sample are still subject to parental control and restraint, whether at home or away at school. Fifty-three percent still live at home, and another fifth live in the same neighborhood or city as their parents.

Further opportunity for social control of the Sansei by the older generation is provided by non-parental relatives. Eighty-three percent of the Sansei sample have at least one relative in the same city or county. In addition, one-quarter have nonnuclear relations right in the home, primarily with grandparents. The degree of Sansei interaction with kin is further indicated by the claim of three in every four that they pay regular visits to nonhousehold relatives. In fact, one-third visit five or more times a month. Table 4.9 reports that, for the present at least, the visiting pattern virtually mirrors that of their parents.

Despite the opportunity by the Nisei to censor Sansei behavior or to reinforce their affiliation with their ethnic community, the Sansei differ markedly from their elders in many respects. For example, religious affiliation (or lack of it) does bespeak certain tendencies toward acculturation. Of the Issei grandparents, 65 percent were Buddhist, and 35 percent were converted to Christianity or were (in minute ratios) born into a Christian family. The Nisei figures are: 37 percent, Buddhist; 54 percent, Christian; and 9 percent, nonbelievers. The Sansei continue the trend: 24 percent adhere to Buddhism and 56 percent to Christianity, while 20 percent profess no faith at all.

Other studies have reported comparative figures for religious affiliation. In contrast to our findings, Connor reports that the religious faith of the Nisei can be listed as being predominantly Buddhist.[33] Sixty-six percent of the female and 64 percent of the male Nisei were adherents. The remainder of Connor's Nisei respondents list themselves as Christian Protestants. Connor's study reveals that almost 50 percent of both male and female Sansei report being Buddhist. Thirty-nine percent of the females and 33 percent of the males report Christianity as their faith, while the remainder gave "agnostic" or "no religion" as their response. Thus whereas Connor reports a gradual decline in the percentage of Japanese Americans who identify themselves as Buddhists (70 percent of the Issei, some 60 percent of the Nisei, down to about 50 percent of the Sansei), our findings (reported in Table 4.9) reveal a dramatic drop from 65 percent of the Issei to 37 percent of the Nisei and down to 24 percent of the Sansei. Regarding church attendance, Kitano and Kiefer found that the highest rate of attendance was by the Issei, followed by the Nisei, then by the Sansei.[34] This would appear to coincide with our trend data showing a lessening of religious affiliation by generation.

In sum, the data from both historical sources and recent empirical studies indicate that the Issei brought with them to the United States a flexible approach to religion. Kitano indicates that most had gone through no baptismal or confirmation ritual and were not churchgoers, although most came from a broadly Buddhist background that influenced the ceremonial aspects of birth, marriage, and death.[35] Otherwise, the focus of any religious training was ethical behavior—how one acted toward parents, friends, and strangers. In general, the Japanese are tolerant of all theologies and, in many cases, tend to adopt the religion of the country in which they find themselves. Miyamoto's survey of Seattle found most Japanese there claiming to be Protestants, and later data gathered among the Japanese in Brazil found most of them to be Catholic.[36]

The adoption of the Christian faith by the Japanese in the United States was in many respects influenced by practical considerations. Christian churches offered much to the new immigrant in the way of Americanization and even employment.[37] Daniels has noted that even among the Buddhist Issei, their religion became Americanized to such an extent that many Protestant hymns were adopted almost word for word.[38] Because of this flexible approach it would appear that religion is not a good measure of acculturation for the Japanese.

As we reported earlier, the present-day Japanese American neighborhood is not a ghetto; the population is too thin. Thus, 45 percent of even the Issei live in neighborhoods that are largely non-Japanese American, as do 58 percent of all Nisei surveyed. As expected, the Sansei live in neighborhoods that are even more alien: 67 percent of our Sansei respondents live among other ethnic groups, mostly Caucasian (see Table 4.9). This neighborhood mixture would serve to counteract traditional pressures from the older generations. Kiefer has noted, for example, that although both Nisei and Sansei are familiar with the workings of American society, the Nisei seem to emphasize proper behavior while the Sansei seem to sense the meanings behind social forms to a greater extent.[39] This has led to misunderstandings between the generations.

Apart from family and neighbors, more formal associations can act as agencies of social control. Of the Nisei who belong to at least one formal organization, fully 45 percent report that they devote the majority of their leisure time to a Japanese American group. In contrast, only 31 percent of the Sansei choose a Japanese American organization as their favorite (Table 4.9). Again we observe a movement away from that which is distinctively ethnic among the younger Japanese Americans.

Education and Occupational Choice

As we have reported elsewhere, Japanese Americans have a phenomenal record for educational accomplishment.[40] According to Kitano, one of the strongest expectations to be carried over from Japan was the belief that higher education was the ticket to a higher level of income and social status.[41] The Japanese sacrificed in order to take advantage of every educational opportunity open to them in the United States. Kramer, likewise, has noted that "Japanese immigrants . . . valued education as a channel of mobility and stressed it in the socialization of their children; this obtained, whatever their class. They consequently achieved even more than members of the dominant group."[42]

In terms of median school years they do have the highest rate of any population group reported by the Census, white or nonwhite. This is reflected within our study. Fifty-seven percent of the Nisei queried have had at least some college training. The Sansei continue the trend: a remarkable 88 percent have gone beyond high school. And the figures are nearly as high for women as for men.

What are the occupational aspirations of the men in the Sansei sample, most of whom were still in college when our questionnaire arrived?[43] Over seven in every ten would choose a profession as the preferred life's work. This contrasts with their grandparents' goal of owning a small farm or business and with their parents' preference for white collar jobs.[44]

Seventy-two percent of the Sansei are certain they will achieve their occupational goal or find it highly likely. Six in ten see a profession as a likely occupation. Professionalism, then, is well established among Sansei as most desirable. While they believe they have the chance to achieve it, only 5 percent of the Issei and 32 percent of the Nisei could reach so favored a socioeconomic position. Kitano has concluded that because of the changing occupational expectations, we can expect to see subtle changes in the social-class structure, generation by generation.[45] Of interest to us, however, in terms of the maintenance of the Japanese American community, are the specific professions to which the young Sansei men aspire.

Sansei Occupational Preference

Consideration of the specific occupations preferred by the Sansei in our sample reveals that 73 percent of the Sansei men plan to enter a profession and that a sizable proportion of these have chosen fields that would separate them from the immediate confines of a local Japanese American community. Specifically, 42 percent of the respondents plan to enter fields like engineering, science, and college teaching. Requirements of the labor market would blindly disperse them across the land to locales relatively empty of Japanese Americans. The others select professions (medicine, dentistry, and accounting, for example) that would permit a return to familiar environs once training was completed. Of the men whose profession would carry a tendency toward dispersal, 94 percent choose some branch of engineering, the sciences, or the humanities. The largest cluster is in engineering, which attracts about one in every five of those in this classification.

Kitano observes that "as the Japanese grow in affluence, we would expect their children to choose college majors that are less concretely job-oriented and more often involved with the liberal arts, social sciences, and literature. We would expect more to leave the West Coast."[46]

Sansei Outmarriage

Perhaps the most telling findings regarding the movement of the Sansei relate to their marriages and marriage plans. Only 30 percent of our sample are married. Of the married, 40 percent married a non-Japanese. As already reported, this compares to only 10 percent of the Nisei who have been exogamous, and only 1 percent of the Issei.

Among the single Sansei, 6 percent are engaged and 29 percent are "going steady" while the rest are dating casually or not dating at all. Of those Sansei who are engaged or going steady, 55 percent are involved with non-Japanese Americans, usually Caucasians. We can safely predict that the outmarriage rate will be even greater among the subgeneration of Sansei — those too young to have been surveyed in 1967-1968. Only 10 percent of respondents say that outmarriage is bad and 74 percent are indifferent about outmarriage. If this trend continues it will surely spell the weakening, if not the dissolution, of the Japanese American community within one or two generations. As Kiefer has stated, "More and more Sansei are marrying outside the ethnic community . . . indicating a greater autonomy in their choice of life style that stems from their ability to melt into affluent American society."[47]

In another study of Japanese American outmarriage in Los Angeles, Fresno, San Francisco, and Hawaii, Kikumura and Kitano concluded that the Japanese are no longer a group that marries their own.[48] Instead they conclude that Japanese in these four areas are now choosing marital partners as much without as within their racial group. Rates of interracial marriage follow a historical pattern that initially showed a high and almost exclusive preference for other Japanese. This pattern changed in the second (or Nisei) generation and has reached the 50 percent level by the third (or Sansei) generation. Kikumura and Kitano hypothesize that this rate will continue to grow with each new successive generation, so that in time there may no longer be a "pure" Japanese American group.

As reported earlier in this chapter, we found that, for the Nisei, outmarriage was one of our most useful indicators for predicting disaffiliation with the Japanese American community. We expect that this same variable will work in a similar fashion for the four in ten Sansei who have outmarried. What are the stresses and strains upon these outmarried Sansei? Have they been ostracized or rebuked by their kin? Or has their choice of a non-Japanese American mate not affected their ethnic affiliation? Since outmarriage seems to be a very salient variable in predicting the assimilation of ethnic groups, we turn now to look at the effects of Sansei outmarriage upon ethnic ties.

Sansei Outmarriage by Sex. Table 4.10 reports the relationship between Sansei outmarriage and sex. We find no association between outmarriage and sex. Approximately four in ten of either sex are exogamous. Similarly, we find only a negligible association between sex and exogamy for their Nisei parents.

Sansei Outmarriage by Age. We find quite a different relationship between age and outmarriage. Table 4.10 reports that there is a moderate negative relationship between the two (gamma = -.44). We find that the youngest Sansei (18 to 20 years) are more than twice as likely to outmarry than their peers 25 years or older. Stated another way, almost seven in ten of the youngest Sansei have outmarried as compared to only three in ten of their oldest peers, even though the age range is not great. This finding con-

Table 4.10

Sansei Endogamy and Exogamy by Measures of Socioeconomic Status

	Spouse Ethnicity				
	Japanese	Non-Japanese	%	N	Gamma
Sex					+.03
Male	61%	39	100%	(94)	
Female	59%	41	100%	(144)	
Age					−.44
18 to 20 years	33%	67	100%	(15)	
21 to 24 years	48%	52	100%	(89)	
25 years or older	70%	30	100%	(132)	

firms our expectation that the subgeneration of younger Sansei would tend to be less inculcated with Japanese tradition.

Sansei Outmarriage by Ethnicity of Neighborhood. In terms of neighborhood ethnicity, Table 4.11 shows that only a quarter of the outmarried Sansei live among other Japanese Americans as compared with one-third of those who married within the ethnic fold. There are two possible sequences behind this finding. One sequence might be that prior to marriage the exogamous Sansei lived in a non-Japanese neighborhood, either near or with his Nisei parents, and after marriage merely took up residence in another Caucasian neighborhood. Or alternatively, upon marriage outside the ethnic fold, the Sansei felt rebuked by his family and the Japanese American community at large, and therefore was no longer comfortable living in a Japanese American neighborhood. Unfortunately, given that our sample is cross-sectional rather than longitudinal, our data can shed no light on which of the sequences is more prevalent.

Sansei Outmarriage by Residence Among Relatives. We find that in terms of living within the same metropolitan area as one's relatives, about three in ten of the Sansei who outmarry tend to be

Table 4.11

Sansei Endogamy and Exogamy by Measures of Community Affiliation

	Spouse Ethnicity		
	Japanese	Non-Japanese	Gamma
Neighborhood ethnicity			+.18
Japanese American and other ethnic groups	34	26	
Non-Japanese American	66	74	
	100%	100%	
	(142)	(96)	
Number of relatives living in same city or county?			-.38
None	11	31	
One to four	13	16	
Five to fourteen	32	27	
Fifteen or more	44	26	
	100%	100%	
	(135)	(96)	
Number of relatives living in neighborhood?			-.30
None	65	78	
One to two	9	8	
Three to six	15	8	
Seven or more	11	5	
	100%	99%	
	(139)	(96)	

Table 4.11 (Continued)

	Japanese	Non-Japanese	Gamma
Number of monthly visits with relatives?			-.44
None	11	34	
One to four	39	36	
Five or more	50	30	
	100%	100%	
	(134)	(88)	
Do you want your children to take an active part with Caucasians in their activities?			-.41
Yes, with Caucasians	75	87	
Associate with both Japanese Americans and Caucasians	10	11	
No, stick with Japanese Americans	15	2	
	100%	100%	
	(141)	(94)	
Do you know the name of the prefecture in Japan from which your grand- parents immigrated?			+.55
Yes	69	38	
No	31	62	
	100%	100%	
	(140)	(91)	

Table 4.11 (Continued)

	Japanese	Non-Japanese	Gamma
Attitude toward intermarriage with Caucasians			-.69
Good	8	26	
Indifferent	75	73	
Bad	17	1	
	100%	100%	
	(139)	(91)	
Should minority groups try to preserve some of their culture or blend into the mainstream of American society?			+.21
Preserve	68	59	
Blend	32	41	
	100%	100%	
	(142)	(92)	
Ethnicity of two closest friends			-.69
One or both non-Japanese	58	87	
Both Japanese	42	13	
	100%	100%	
	(139)	(93)	
Membership in Japanese American organization			-.70
None	78	96	
One	18	2	
Two or more	4	2	
	100%	100%	
	(142)	(95)	

Table 4.11 (Continued)

	Japanese	Non-Japanese	Gamma
Ethnic membership of favorite organization			+.62
Japanese American	27	8	
Non-Japanese American	73	92	
	100%	100%	
	(48)	(25)	
Religion			+.57
Buddhist	43	13	
Christian	47	61	
Non-believer	10	26	
	100%	100%	
	(140)	(92)	
Read Japanese American newspapers			+.58
Regularly	11	4	
Occasionally	38	15	
Never	51	81	
	100%	100%	
	(142)	(96)	
Speaks Japanese			+.36
Quite fluently	4	4	
Pretty well	19	6	
Only a little	54	49	
Not at all	23	40	
	100%	100%	
	(142)	(95)	

isolates as compared with only one in ten of the endogamous (Table 4.11). Similarly, at the neighborhood level, almost eight in ten exogamous Sansei do not live among any relatives, compared with six in ten of the endogamous.

Sansei Outmarriage by Visiting Patterns. When we look at a behavioral indicator of affiliation—monthly visiting with relatives—there is a similar pattern. Table 4.11 reveals that three in ten of the exogamous Sansei are isolates and only one in ten of them endogamous. Whether this is by choice or by rebuke from relatives is unknown. But it is incontrovertible that the ties are looser for the exogamous. At the opposite end of the visiting pattern—those who visit often (five or more times per month)—again it is the endogamous who visit more frequently. Five in ten visit that frequently in comparison to three in ten of their outmarried peers.

We thus find a consistent difference between the endogamous and the exogamous. What is the time order of events? Do those Sansei who outmarry move away from things Japanese and reduce community ties even before marriage? Or is it that outmarriage produces a negative reaction among the relatives, encouraging voluntary or imposed exclusion? Of course, it may be that the two processes work jointly to reinforce one another.

The remainder of the findings in Table 4.11 sheds some light on this question of time order of events. On each of the items that serve to measure either ethnocentric attitudes, practices, or knowledge, we find that it is the exogamous who consistently reveal evidence of a movement away from things Japanese.

The exogamous, for example, are least likely to want their children to socialize solely with other Japanese Americans. Rather, they want their children to take an active part in the activities of Caucasians. Similarly, in the area of historical knowledge of their grandparents' prefecture of origin, fewer than four in ten of the exogamous as compared to almost seven in ten of the endogamous know the name of the prefecture. Regarding the question of intermarriage with Caucasians, over one in six (17 percent) endogamous Sansei report that it is a "bad" idea, whereas only a scant 1 percent of the exogamous report the same attitude.

Consistent with these findings, Obidinski found several important attitudinal and behavioral differences between second and third generation Polish residents of Buffalo, New York, including increasing approval of ethnic intermarriage (38 percent to 64 percent, respectively), decreasing support for a political candidate solely on the basis of Polish-American identity (85 percent to 65 percent, respectively), and decreasing preference for use of the Polish language during the entire Roman Catholic service (67 percent to 31 percent, respectively).[49]

When we asked the Sansei whether minority groups in American society should attempt to preserve something of their cultures, or whether they should blend in with the mainstream of American society, four in ten of the exogamous and three in ten of the endogamous favor assimilation. This is not a great difference, but the direction is consistent with our other findings.

Similarly, with regard to ethnicity of two closest friends, almost six in ten of the endogamous Sansei have one or more non-Japanese as their two closest friends, while the proportion of exogamous Sansei in this position is almost nine in ten. As with the Nisei there seems to be a greater tendency among the exogamous Sansei to move away from the Japanese community than is true for their endogamous peers. We suspect these friendship choices are related to the fact that most Sansei are presently on college campuses, which of course enroll largely non-Japanese students. Consequently, simple probability factors are at work that can influence ethnicity of friendship choices. At some colleges there may be so few Sansei that they are foreclosed from commingling and must seek out Caucasian friends.

In terms of organizational memberships, too, we find that the exogamous Sansei are less likely to belong to any Japanese American organizations. If they do belong to one, it is not likely to be that organization to which they devote most of their leisure time.

Finally, when we look at other cultural links with institutions of the Japanese American community — religion, Japanese American newspaper readership, and language — we find in each case that the exogamous tend to be less Japanese. Exogamous Sansei, for example, are less likely to retain their traditional religion, Buddhism. Only about one in ten of the exogamous Sansei are Buddhists, as against over four in ten of their endogamous peers. In another indication of the transition the exogamous are apparently making, we find that over twice as many exogamous as endogamous Sansei report having no religious affiliation whatever (26 percent and 10 percent, respectively). At this point it is important to recall that historically the Japanese have had a pluralistic outlook in regard to religion.[50]

Consistent with our findings, Lopata's study of the Polish community found that church attendance varies by generation.[51] The second generation was much more likely than the third to report going to church several times a week (36 percent of the second as compared to 4 percent of the third generation). Lopata hypothesizes that decreasing identification with Polonia in each succeeding generation may lead to a decrease of association membership and community participation in general. That is, Polonia developed because of the active participation of the first generation of all social classes. It has continued with the help of the established higher classes of both emigrations. The third generation, although already in the middle class, seems to be less involved in the community life and status competition and may, simultaneously, be decreasing organizational and community involvement. Lopata concludes that her finding (the higher the class, the lower the association involvement) is a reversal of American trends.[52]

In another study of Polish Americans, Sandberg indicates that the West Coast has tended to draw a more assimilated or higher class Polish American (note the correlation of the two) into secondary settlement.[53] Sandberg's study of the Polish-American community in Los Angeles revealed that with each generation of Polish Americans, membership in Polish parishes, and in any church for that matter, has declined. In general, there were few differences in ethnicity and behavior between the third and fourth generations. The greatest amounts of decreasing ethnicity (as measured by Sandberg) were between the first and second generations, modified considerably by ethnic class.

We find similar results concerning the readership of Japanese American newspapers, such as the official organ of the Japanese American Citizens League, *The Pacific Citizen*. Fewer than two in ten of the exogamous ever read a Japanese American newspaper, as compared with almost five in ten of the endogamous. The same difference is apparent in the Sansei's Japanese language fluency.

Whereas four in ten of the exogamous cannot speak Japanese at all, this is true for only two in ten of the endogamous.

The data presented in Table 4.11 indicate, then, that the process by which outmarriage occurs among the Sansei includes a growing movement away from ties with their community in terms of ethnicity of residence, closeness to relatives, organizational membership, and friendship choices.

In summary, for almost every indicator of the maintenance of the Japanese American community, we have seen that the Sansei have moved further away from the ethnic community than the Nisei. Furthermore, this process is particularly accelerated among the exogamous Sansei. It seems likely that the Sansei have one foot in both cultures and may be fully accepted by neither. In this sense they would indeed be marginal members of either group.

We would expect still deeper reductions of affiliation with the next, or Yonsei, generation as they come of age within two decades. In the next chapter we offer a prognosis for the future of the Japanese American community, based upon the data we have collected.

Notes

1. Jessie Bernard, *The Sociology of Community*; and Stanford M. Lyman, "Contrasts in the Community Organization of Chinese and Japanese in North America."
2. Gerhard Lenski, *The Religious Factor*, pp. 214-217.
3. Ibid.
4. For reviews of findings, see Bernard Barber, *Social Stratification*, pp. 418-421; Stanley Lieberson, "The Impact of Residential Segregation on Ethnic Assimilation"; Seymour M. Lipset and Reinhard Bendix, *Social Mobility in Industrial Society*, pp. 157-164; Robert K. Merton, *Social Theory and Social Structure*, pp. 400-401; and Robert P. Stuckert, "Occupational Mobility and Family Relationships."
5. Lenski, *The Religious Factor*, pp. 214-217.
6. Sheila R. Klatzky, *Patterns of Contact with Relatives*, p. 84.
7. Helena Znaniecki Lopata, *Polish Americans*, p. 109.
8. Joan W. Moore, *Mexican Americans*, 2nd ed., p. 137.
9. Steven Martin Cohen, "Socioeconomic Determinants of Intraethnic Marriage and Friendship," p. 1003.

10. Ibid., pp. 997-1010.

11. Klatzky, *Patterns of Contact with Relatives*, p. 85.

12. Bert N. Adams, *Kinship in an Urban Setting*, p. 169.

13. Edna M. Bonacich, "Small Business and Japanese American Ethnic Solidarity."

14. Unfortunately, we collected occupational data only for the male Nisei.

15. Klatzky, *Patterns of Contact with Relatives*, p. 84.

16. Ibid.

17. J. M. Bruce, "Intragenerational Occupational Mobility and Visiting with Kin and Friend," p. 126.

18. Lenski, *The Religious Factor*, p. 214.

19. David M. Schneider and George C. Homans, "Kinship Terminology and the American Kinship System."

20. Fred L. Strodtbeck, "Family Interaction, Values and Achievement," pp. 147-165.

21. Adams, *Kinship in an Urban Setting*, p. 170.

22. Ibid., p. 171; Schneider and Homans, "Kinship Terminology and the American Kinship System."

23. In order to maintain consistency in the interpretation of values for Gamma, this author will employ the following useful criteria set forth in James A. Davis, *Elementary Survey Analysis*, p. 49: .01 to .09 = a negligible association; .10 to .29 = a low association; .30 to .49 = a moderate association; .50 to .69 = a substantial association; and .70 to 1.0 = a very strong association.

24. John W. Connor, *Tradition and Change in Three Generations of Japanese Americans*, p. 104.

25. For reviews of findings, see M. Barron, *The Blending Americans, Patterns of Intermarriage*; Cohen, "Socioeconomic Determinants of Intraethnic Marriage and Friendship"; Milton Gordon, *Assimilation in American Life*; Robert K. Merton, "Intermarriage and Social Structure"; John N. Tinker, "Intermarriage and Ethnic Boundaries."

26. Gordon, *Assimilation in American Life*, p. 80.

27. U.S. Bureau of the Census, *Marital Status*, p. 262.

28. Ibid.

29. Romanzo C. Adams, *Interracial Marriage in Hawaii*; and Andrew W. Lind, *Hawaii's People*, 3rd ed.

30. For reviews of findings, see M. Hansen, "The Third Generation in America"; Will Herberg, *Protestant, Catholic, Jew*; and George Kagiwada, "The Third Generation Hypothesis."

31. Christie Kiefer, *Changing Cultures, Changing Lives*, p. 104.

32. Ibid., pp. 106-108.

33. Connor, *Tradition and Change in Three Generations of Japanese Americans*, p. 105.

34. Harry H. L. Kitano, *Japanese Americans*, 2nd ed., pp. 114-116; and Kiefer, *Changing Cultures, Changing Lives*, p. 34.

35. Kitano, *Japanese Americans*, 2nd ed., p. 58.

36. S. Frank Miyamoto, "Social Solidarity among the Japanese in Seattle"; and Office of Population Research, "Japanese Immigrants in Brazil," p. 136.

37. Kitano, *Japanese Americans*, 2nd ed., p. 59.

38. Roger Daniels, *The Politics of Prejudice*, pp. 14-15.

39. Kiefer, *Changing Cultures, Changing Lives*.

40. Gene N. Levine and Darrel Montero, "Socioeconomic Mobility among Three Generations of Japanese Americans."

41. Kitano, *Japanese Americans*, 2nd ed.

42. Judith R. Kramer, *The American Minority Community*, p. 102.

43. Data regarding female Sansei occupational choices were not available for analysis.

44. Kitano, *Japanese Americans*, 2nd ed., p. 99.

45. Ibid.

46. Ibid., p. 98.

47. Kiefer, *Changing Cultures, Changing Lives*, p. 116.

48. Akemi Kikumura and Harry H. L. Kitano, "Interracial Marriage."

49. Eugene Obidinski, "Ethnic to Status Group."

50. Kitano, *Japanese Americans*, 2nd ed.

51. Helena Znaniecki Lopata, *Polish Americans*.

52. Ibid., p. 109.

53. Neil C. Sandberg, *Ethnic Identity and Assimilation*.

5

Summary and Conclusions: Prospects for the Maintenance of the Japanese American Community

A Review of the Study

Our inquiry began as a two-pronged effort. First, we set out to describe the mainland Japanese as a distinctive American minority group and thereto presented a pertinent social profile. We observed that Japanese Americans number just over one-half million, including Hawaii. And, although Japanese Americans now reside in every one of the fifty states, we showed this to be a recent, postwar phenomenon. In 1960, twenty-three states had 1,000 or more Japanese American residents, and even these were relatively new arrivals, since in 1940 there were only seven states that had 1,000 or more residents. Even with postwar dispersion from the Pacific Coast, Figure 4.1 shows that the Japanese are still heavily concentrated on the West Coast. All told, there are five major centers of concentration across the country: Los Angeles, San Francisco, Seattle, Chicago, and New York City.

After noting their concentration, we turned secondly to a discussion of the Japanese American socioeconomic status. According to the 1970 Census, Japanese Americans have the highest level of educational attainment among white and nonwhite groups alike. Their median family income is nearly $4,000 above the median U.S. family income. With respect to occupational status, their achievements are notable. We find that the Japanese Americans, according to 1970 Census data, are much more likely to be employed as professionals than the U.S. population at large. While it is important to remember that these statistics may not accurately reflect the conditions in which individual Japanese

Americans may find themselves, it is nevertheless evident that as a group they have fared better in this society than most other ethnic minorities.

Out of this evidence of socioeconomic achievement emerged the following query: What impact has the economic advancement of Japanese Americans had upon the cohesiveness and solidarity of their ethnic community, which has apparently been so instrumental to their success? Does departure from the community (geographically, psychologically, or both) smooth the road to success? In short, what is the relationship between socioeconomic advancement and assimilation into the larger American society?

As an initial response to our question we found that since 1915 a declining proportion of Japanese Americans live in predominantly Japanese American neighborhoods. This figure has fallen systematically from a high of 30 percent in 1915 to a tiny 4 percent of our Nisei respondents in 1967. The majority (58 percent) now live in predominantly non-Japanese neighborhoods. Still, four in ten of the Nisei live among some compatriots.

With regard to the character of the ethnically mixed communities, our findings are inconsistent. On the one hand, nearly one in every five respondents is an isolate who does not live closely even to one relative. On the other hand, half of the Nisei live in the same city with five or more of their relatives. At the neighborhood level, too, about half live among some relatives. We can state that a bare majority of the Nisei are still potentially affiliated with their community in the sense that they have at least the opportunity to associate with relatives.

But does presence of kin lead to interaction? We found (Table 4.4) that of those who have relatives in the same metropolitan area, a relatively large percentage (one-third) choose *not* to visit them regularly. To a surprising degree, the fact that related Japanese Americans live in the same locality is no guarantee of association. The figure may indicate some breakdown of ethnic tradition.

Using organizational membership as another measure of community affiliation, we found that 57 percent of the Nisei belong to no Japanese American organization. And of those who do belong, fewer than half consider a Japanese American organization their favorite. In addition, almost one-half have no personal knowledge of an ethnic community leader. And finally, regarding one of our most telling measures of community affiliation, we found that over one-half of the Nisei report that one or both of their two closest friends are non-Japanese.

Our study focused upon four basic indicators of assimilation for the Japanese American community in the United States: (1) visiting patterns with relatives, (2) ethnicity of favorite organization, (3) ethnicity of two closest friends, and (4) rate of intermarriage. The independent variables used to examine these indicators of assimilation were sex, age, occupation, and education. Let us now review some of the major empirical generalizations that we have found and their theoretical implications.

We found very little systematic relationship between age and visiting patterns with relatives, and almost no relationship by sex. Occupation and education are inversely related to visiting with relatives. That is, the higher the occupational and educational status that our Nisei has attained, the less likely it is that he will visit with his relatives. This finding coincides with Strodtbeck's study of Italian Catholics and Jewish families in New Haven, Connecticut, which revealed that the greater economic success of the Jews was linked with their willingness to leave kith and kin.[1]

The theoretical implication of this reduction in extended family visiting patterns again suggests that as the Japanese Americans continue to move up the socioeconomic ladder, the very mortar that serves to cement together the ethnic community may begin to crumble. This phenomenon has profound implications for the maintenance of the Japanese American community. It is possible that the ethnic community may have hastened its own demise by that very support that it has provided in order to enable its members to advance socioeconomically.

The relationship of our four major independent variables to organizational affiliation was similar to that found for other measures of assimilation. Our findings show that the youngest Nisei (aged thirty-three and younger) are almost twice as likely as their elders (fifty-three years and older) to choose a non-Japanese organization as their favorite. We expected females, as the important culture carriers, to show a greater preference than males for ethnic organizations. Our findings, however, indicate that the reverse is the case. Women are in fact somewhat *less* likely than men to list a Japanese organization as their favorite. Occupation and education are directly related to choice of organizational affiliation. Only two out of ten of those with postgraduate level education selected an ethnic organization as their favorite, while some six out of ten of those with a high school education or less chose a Japanese organization. Similarly, eight out of ten of the service workers preferred ethnic organizations, as opposed to only three out of ten of the professional respondents.

Theoretical implications seem to suggest a marked trend away from Japanese affiliation on this indicator also. That is, it is the youngest Nisei who are least likely to belong to Japanese American organizations. Also, the higher the occupational and educational standing, the less likely are the Nisei to maintain a Japanese American organizational affiliation. Most importantly, it is the postgraduates who have dramatically moved away from choosing Japanese American organizations as their favorites. These findings have important theoretical implications as the Japanese continue to move up the socioeconomic ladder, and suggests a further deterioration or at least movement away from Japanese affiliations and traditions.

We found no essential difference between male and female Nisei in their choice of closest friends. Younger Nisei were much more likely than their elders to list non-Japanese as their closest friends. Their occupation and education probably affect this choice, the younger Nisei usually having a higher educational and occupational status. Occupation and education are positively related to Caucasian friendship choice. That is, the higher the occupational and educational attainment, the more likely it is that the Nisei will choose a Caucasian as his or her best friend. Similarly, a study by Cohen using a national sample showed that immigrant groups who had been in the United States the longest were more likely to claim interethnic friendships than were new immigrants.[2]

These findings have considerable theoretical implications. If this relationship between occupation, education, and friendship choice continues, then our respondents' ever increasing socioeconomic mobility will spell the weakening of intraethnic friendship ties among Japanese Americans. It may in fact further promote outside friendships at the expense of intraethnic ties. These newly established relationships would have important implications for racial intermarriage. For example, if Nisei have largely Caucasian friends, these friends and their offspring will have considerable impact upon the Nisei's offspring, the Sansei. As entire families visit each other, they become agents of peer group socialization. Eventually, this would be likely to influence their choice in mate selection.

Contrary to our expectations, we found no relationship between sex and outmarriage. Age, however, was found to be inversely related to outmarriage. That is, the younger the Nisei, the more likely he or she is to marry a non-Japanese. We have seen that occupation and education are positively related to racial intermarriage. The higher the occupational and educational achievement the more likely are the Nisei to choose to marry outside the ethnic fold. Thus it becomes evident that each indicator of increasing socioeconomic status points to an increasing rate of intermarriage.

Women have traditionally been considered to be the main bearers of Japanese culture. They retain Buddhist affiliation and speak and read Japanese more fluently than their male counterparts. Because of this, we expected their rate of assimilation to lag behind that of the Japanese male. Our study, however, revealed some inconsistent findings. We found no essential differences by sex in visiting patterns with relatives, ethnicity of favorite organization, and choice of friends and marriage partner.

Nisei and Sansei Differential Community Affiliation

On many levels of affiliation we find that the Nisei and Sansei differ quite markedly. In terms of number of relatives in the same neighborhood or ethnicity of neighborhood, the Sansei are somewhat more likely to be ethnically cut off than the Nisei (Table 4.9). Using additional indicators such as ethnicity of two closest friends, religious affiliation, reading of Japanese American newspapers, ethnicity of favorite organization, and spouse ethnicity, we found more dramatic differences. The Sansei are clearly moving away from Japanese concerns. Three in four have non-Japanese as closest friends, compared with only one-half of the Nisei. Similarly, only one Sansei in every four adheres to the traditional religion of Buddhism, as against one in three of the

Nisei. On the matter of keeping informed about the community, only one in seven of the Sansei reads Japanese American newspapers regularly, as compared with over one in three of the preceding generation.

The ethnic flavor of the favorite organization follows the same pattern. Among those Sansei who are members of any organization, only one in three choose a Japanese American organization, as against almost one in two of the Nisei. Lopata's study of Polish-American organizational affiliation reveals the same general pattern.[3] Her findings indicate that 50 percent of the first generation, 42 percent of the second, and only 30 percent of the third generation belong to a Polish organization. Moreover, the third generation is much less active in voluntary organizations, both Polish and purely American, than are prior generations.

Perhaps the most telling indicator of what is to come is the difference in rates of exogamy between the generations. Only one in ten of the Nisei had chosen to outmarry, compared to four in ten of those Sansei respondents who had wed by the time of this study's field work. Further, we have seen that when we looked at the endogamous and exogamous Sansei, we learned that it was the exogamous who were higher on each indicator of assimilation. We believe that it is the increasing outmarriage rate that will have the greatest impact on the form of the Japanese American community. It is the outmarried Sansei who are moving away from things Japanese.

As reported in Table 4.11, when we cross-tabulated Sansei spouse ethnicity by measures of community affiliation, without exception we found that the exogamous, to a much greater extent than the endogamous, are moving away from Japanese culture, institutions, and affiliations. And if the present dating pattern of the youngest subgeneration of Sansei serves as still another indicator, the prognosis for maintenance of community is not good. Our findings indicate that over five in ten are engaged to or dating a non-Japanese. Moreover, interethnic marriages seem to generate their own momentum in the next generation; that is, children of interethnic marriages are more likely to marry individuals outside the ethnic group than offspring of ethnically homogeneous marriages.[4]

The Duality of Attraction Model:
The Unfolding of the Assimilation Process

Underlying the findings produced by our study, we sense a duality of attraction pulling our Japanese American immigrants in two competing directions. That is, there is a desire to preserve one's sense of ethnicity in the face of the pull of socioeconomic advancement. Let us examine a model that seeks to explain the unfolding of this phenomenon.

When the first generation immigrants, the Issei, arrived in the United States, they sought (and found) security within the ethnic enclave. Regarding themselves as sojourners, they came to the United States in search of financial security, and planned to return to their homeland once they made their fortunes.[5] They settled in ghettos, comforted by the similarity of language, custom, and culture. They organized according to prefecture of origin, and formed ethnic institutions as systems of mutual aid and support, such as rotating credit associations.[6]

An ethnic economy was formed, composed of small shopkeepers and proprietorships that served the Japanese American community. The ethnic economy served to hold together the Japanese American community, to reinforce values, customs, behavior, and social control.[7]

The value system of the Japanese encouraged economic success, which is one reason why they came to the United States in the first place.[8] Solidly entrenched within the ethnic community, those who did not find suitable employment within the ethnic economy were ready to branch out into the larger Anglo society in search of financial success. Like it or not, he or she had to learn the language, customs, habits, and practices of the host society in order to make headway and gain an economic foothold in that newly adopted society. Through hard work and perseverance, aided as well by their value system, which was compatible with that of the American middle class, they soon achieved a measure of financial security.[9] This allowed them to send their children, the Nisei, to universities and other institutions of higher education.

Finding themselves on heterogeneous college campuses with few other Japanese students, the Nisei necessarily formed friendships with non-Japanese. Their educational achievements opened the door to higher occupational status than had been possible for their parents. The Japanese value system holds family and tradition very dear, and our Nisei were confronted with a difficult decision: a duality of attraction. They were feeling the lure of economic advancement from the host American society, while feeling the conflicting pull of alternative employment offered by the ethnic economy. Those who chose to become doctors or lawyers, for instance, could choose to serve the ethnic community or to practice their profession within the adopted American society. On the other hand, those who chose to become engineers, teachers, and business executives found that advancement in those fields required geographical mobility.

Since geographic mobility is generally required to achieve economic advancement, this entailed a willingness to leave kith and kin to seek one's fortune. This is the tipping point, as it were: when the social-psychological value and comfort provided by the ethnic community begin to diminish in relative terms to the lure of the socioeconomic advancement that higher education now allows.

There may be no going back once this tipping point is reached. Furthermore, even where there is a desire to return to the ethnic fold, the socioeconomic advantages of "tipping over" make it difficult to do anything but that. Originally, ethnic cohesion was an advantage in that it helped the Japanese to gain a foothold in American society. In contrast, affiliation with the ethnic community for the Nisei now becomes a relative disadvantage to getting ahead in their present environment.

Economic success encourages movement from Little Tokyos and Japan Towns into the surrounding suburbs, thus splintering community ties. The process of assimilation may be accelerated by the absence of the Issei, who have remained in the ethnic enclave and are no longer present to ensure that their grandchildren, the Sansei, receive a traditional Japanese upbringing. If the Sansei are reared in largely non-Japanese American communities, the absence of other Japanese children to serve as agents of socialization will further speed the assimilation process.

Another salient factor that contributes to the assimilation of the Nisei is that they do not consider themselves sojourners as did their parents, the Issei.[10] They have known only the United States as home and may wish consciously to assimilate. As the Nisei succeed in occupations that require them to live in largely non-Japanese communities, they form friendships and professional acquaintances among Caucasians. These newly established relationships have important implications for racial intermarriage and ultimately for their complete assimilation into the larger society.

Assimilation and Socioeconomic Status: Implications for the Future

The trend toward greater assimilation is clear. Issei, Nisei, and Sansei rate increasingly higher on every indicator of assimilation. It is apparent that both the Nisei and Sansei are making remarkable strides in socioeconomic advancement, and that advancement in turn is positively related to assimilation. As Kramer observes:

> The ghetto of the first generation, as we have already seen, was organized around the ethnic values of its traditional society; the gilded ghetto of the second generation gave priority to the material values of American society. It is for the third generation to discover the nonmaterial values and to establish a community that encompasses all the elements of prestige enjoyed by the dominant group.[11]

What does the movement away from the Japanese-American community suggest? Can the ethnic community in fact remain intact when its members are being scattered to the four winds as they seek to advance themselves socioeconomically?

Geographical dispersion, economic success, Americanization, and the loss of Japanese skills are interdependent. Upward mobility leads to outward mobility, which leads to increased acculturation.[12] It has likewise been observed that with a continuing emphasis on education, the Sansei would appear to be headed in the direction of even greater socioeconomic success. But it cannot be ignored that continued achievement hinges to some extent upon the availability of appropriate opportunities.[13] In a discussion of American minority communities, Kramer comments that most minority members ultimately remain within the ethnic community only in the face of discrimination from the larger society.[14] Otherwise the temptations of greater economic and political opportunities inevitably pull the minority members into the mainstream of the dominant community.

Our findings suggest that on every indicator of assimilation it is the socioeconomically successful Nisei who are the most cut off from the ethnic community. Since the majority of our Nisei respondents are making considerable economic strides despite evidence of persistent discrimination, this suggests an accelerating rate of assimilation for the Japanese American population as a whole.

Ironically, assimilation itself may suggest the demise of some traditional values of the Japanese American community, which were so instrumental in catapulting its members to these heights. The demise of these values in turn may serve to bring about the leveling off of the Nisei and Sansei's socioeconomic achievement. As their values become more congruent with those of the larger American society, Japanese Americans will most likely begin to mirror the achievement patterns of American society in general. Given the dramatically increasing trend of outmarriage among the Sansei, with its concomitant diminution of ethnic ties and affiliation, we are justified in wondering whether a Japanese American ethnic community can be maintained into the next generation — the Yonsei. If it cannot, it suggests uncertainty for the survival of other distinct ethnic groups as their members advance socioeconomically.

Notes

1. Fred L. Strodtbeck, "Family Interaction, Values, and Achievement."

2. Steven Martin Cohen, "Socioeconomic Determinants of Intraethnic Marriage and Friendship."

3. Helen Znaniecki Lopata, *Polish Americans*.

4. Cohen, "Socioeconomic Determinants of Intraethnic Marriage and Friendship."

5. S. Frank Miyamoto, "Social Solidarity among the Japanese in Seattle."

6. Ivan H. Light, *Ethnic Enterprise in America*.

7. Edna M. Bonacich, "Small Business and Japanese American Ethnic Solidarity."

8. Harry H. L. Kitano, *Japanese Americans*, 2nd ed.

9. Ibid.; William Petersen, "Success Story"; idem, *Japanese Americans*.

10. Miyamoto, "Social Solidarity among the Japanese in Seattle."

11. Judith R. Kramer, *The American Minority Community*, pp. 134-135.

12. Christie Kiefer, *Changing Cultures, Changing Lives*, p. 121.

13. Kitano, *Japanese Americans*, 2nd ed., p. 101.

14. Kramer, *The American Minority Community*, p. 62.

Appendix A:
Nisei Interview Schedule

FOR OFFICE USE ONLY

1 - 9

FOR INTERVIEWER'S USE

National Opinion Research Center
University of Chicago

Survey No. 4013

JAPANESE AMERICAN RESEARCH PROJECT
University of California at Los Angeles

Survey of Japanese Americans:

Phase Two

April, 1967

This survey is supported by a grant from the
U.S. Public Health Service. The directors
of the study assume full responsibility for
the contents of this questionnaire.

```
┌─────────────────────────────────┐
│ ENTER                           │
│ TIME INTERVIEW_____ AM       │
│ BEGAN:              PM          │
└─────────────────────────────────┘
```
                                                                                    BEGIN DECK 01

1. First, we would like to know whether you are single, married, divorced,
   separated, or widowed.

                                                        Single . . 1   10/
                                                        Married . . 2
                                                        Divorced . 3
                                                        Separated . 4
                                                        Widowed . . 5

2. How old were you on your last birthday?

                                                        _____   11-12/

3. Where were you born? _____ _____   13-15/
                              (City)   (State or Country)

4. **ASK MALES ONLY**: Were you the oldest son in your family?   Yes . 1   16/
                                                                  No . 2

5. **ASK EVERYONE**: How many children did your parents have altogether?

                                                        _____   17-18/

ASK Q'S. 6-8 **IF EVER MARRIED**; OTHERWISE SKIP TO Q. 9.

6. Where was your (wife/husband) born?

   _____ _____   19-21/
          (City)   (State or Country)

                                          Don't know. 888

   A. **IF SPOUSE BORN IN U.S.**: What is your (wife/husband)'s background? Is
                                  (she/he) a Nisei, a Sansei, a Caucasian, or of
                                  some other background?

                                  Nisei 1   22/

                                  Sansei 2

                                  Caucasian 3

                                  Japanese (born in Japan) . . 4

                                  Non-Japanese oriental 5

                                  Other (SPECIFY) 6

7. How many children have been born to you and your (wife/husband), not counting
   stillbirths?

                                                        _____   23-24/

8. What kind of work did your father-in-law do when your (wife/husband) was in (her/his) teens?

OCCUPATION: _____ 25-27/
   (PROBE: What did he actually do on that job?)

INDUSTRY: _____

ASK EVERYONE:

9. I'd like to know a few things about some of your other relatives.

	A. (Relative) Living here in this city.		B. Living in your neigh- borhood.		C. Living in this house- hold.	
	Yes	No	Yes	No	Yes	No
A. (1) Do you have any brothers or sisters living in (city/county)?	1	0	1	0	1	0
(2) Do either of your parents live in (city/county)?. . .	2	0	2	0	2	0
(3) And have you any other relatives--including <u>anyone</u> you consider a relative, but not including your own children--living here in (city/county)?	4	0 28/	4	0 31/	4	0 34/

IF YES TO ANY, (1), (2), OR (3),
ASK A (4) AND B.

IF NO TO (1), (2), AND (3), SKIP TO
Q. 11.

(4) About how many relatives does
this make altogether living   City/
in (city/county)? . . . . .   County:_____ Nbrhd:_____ Hshld:_____
                                         29-30/   32-33/   35-36/

B. Now, do any of all these relatives we've talked about live in the same neigh-borhood as you? **IF YES**: Which ones? CIRCLE ALL THAT APPLY [A (1), (2), AND/ OR (3)] UNDER B ABOVE, AND ASK B (1) AND C. **IF NO**: CIRCLE "0'S" IN COLUMN B ABOVE, AND SKIP TO Q. 10.

(1) About how many relatives does this make, who live in your neighborhood? ENTER NUMBER IN TABLE UNDER B ABOVE.

C. And do any of <u>these</u> relatives live with you here in the same household? **IF YES**: Which ones? CIRCLE ALL THAT APPLY UNDER C ABOVE, AND ASK C (1). **IF NO**: CIRCLE "0'S" IN COLUMN C AND SKIP TO Q. 10.

(1) How many relatives live with you in this household? ENTER NUMBER UNDER C.

IF R HAS **ANY** RELATIVES IN CITY, ASK Q. 10.

10. About how many times in the past month have you visited with or been visited by relatives living in (city/county)--(apart from those living in the same household as you)?
                                                        _____ times   37-38/

11. Now about your neighborhood: Do you think of this neighborhood as your real
     home--the place where you really belong, or do you think of it as just a
     place where you happen to be living?

                                        Really belong . 1   39/
                                        Just a place . 2
                                        Don't know . . 8

12. About how many of your neighbors, including relatives, are you on visiting
     terms with?

                                        None 1   40/
                                        One or two . . . 2
                                        Three or four . . 3
                                        Five - nine . . . 4
                                        Ten or more . . . 5
                                        Don't know . . . 8

13. How many years __altogether__ have you lived here in this neighborhood?

                                        Less than 1 year 1   41/
                                        1 to less than 5 years . . 2
                                        5 to less than 10 years . 3
                                        10 to less than 15 years . 4
                                        15 to less than 25 years . 5
                                        25 to less than 35 years . 6
                                        35 years or more 7
                                        All my life 8
                                        Don't know 9

14. Would you say that this neighborhood is made up mostly of Japanese Americans,
     mostly non-Japanese, or is it mixed?

                                        Mostly Japanese Americans. 1   42/
                                        Mixed 2
                                        Mostly non-Japanese . . . 3
                                        Don't know 8

15. What other kinds of groups besides Japanese Americans live in this neighbor-
     hood? DO NOT READ CATEGORIES,
     BUT CIRCLE ALL THAT APPLY.

                    Other orientals (including Filipinos) 01 43-44/
                    Negroes . . . . : . . 02
                    Mexican Americans 03
                    "Caucasians" (no subgroup mentioned) 08
                    Subgroup of Caucasians 16
                    (RECORD; DON'T PROBE FOR ADDITIONAL

                    _____)

                    Others 32
                    (RECORD, DON'T PROBE: _____

                    _____)

                    Don't know 88

16. Now, I'd like to find out about the various cities and towns you've lived in.

A. To start, since when have you lived here in (city/county)?

1967 1	45/
1966 2	
1963 - 1965 3	
1958 - 1962 4	
1953 - 1957 5	
1943 - 1952 6	

ASK B-D FOR EACH PLACE, GOING
BACK TO R'S YEAR OF BIRTH, AND
RECORD BELOW.

Before 1942 7
All my life (GO TO Q. 17) . 8
Don't know 9

B. And in what city or town did you live just before that? City and State, or Country	C. In what year did you move there? Year	D. Were your neighbors there mostly Japanese Americans, mostly non-Japanese, or was the neighborhood mixed?	SPECIAL CODING
1.		J N M	
2.		J N M	
3.		J N M	
4.		J N M	
5.		J N M	
6.		J N M	
7.		J N M	
8.		J N M	
9.		J N M	
10.		J N M	
11.		J N M	
12.		J N M	
13.		J N M	
14.		J N M	
15.		J N M	

17. (You already mentioned this, but let me make sure I got it right.) Were you in a relocation center or camp during World War II?

                                                 Yes . (ASK A) . . . 1   46/
                                                 No (GO TO Q. 18) . 2

   A. IF YES: How long, altogether, did you spend in relocation centers or camps?

                                        Less than 1 year 1   47/
                                        1 to less than 2 years . . . 2
                                        2 to less than 3 years . . . 3
                                        3 to less than 4 years . . . 4
                                        4 to less than 5 years . . . 5
                                        5 years or more 6
                                        Don't know 8

Now, let's talk about (your/your husband's) occupation.

ASK Q'S. 18, 20, 21, AND 22 ABOUT: RESPONDENT IF R IS MALE, OR IF R IS DIVORCED
                                   OR NEVER MARRIED FEMALE;

                                   HUSBAND OF RESPONDENT IF R IS CURRENTLY
                                   MARRIED, WIDOWED, OR SEPARATED FEMALE.

---

18. A. What kind of work (do you/does your husband/did your husband usually) do?

      OCCUPATION:_____ 48-50/
                 [PROBE, IF VAGUE: What (do/does/did) (you/he) actually
                 do on this job?]

   B. In what kind of business or industry (is/was) that?

      BUSINESS OR INDUSTRY:_____
                           (PROBE, IF VAGUE: What does that firm/organ-
                           ization/agency make or do?)

   C. Does that mean (you are/he is) self-employed or employed by someone else?

                                        Self-employed . . . 1   51/
                                        Employed by others . 2
                                        Don't know 8

ASK Q. 19 ONLY ABOUT RESPONDENT; FOR CURRENTLY MARRIED, WIDOWED, OR SEPARATED FE-
MALE, GO TO Q. 20.

19. Is there any other occupation you would prefer to be in?

Yes . (ASK A AND B) . 1   52/

No . (GO TO Q. 20) . . 2

Don't know 8

IF YES:

A. What occupation is that?

OCCUPATION: _____ 53-54/

55/

B. Suppose you were a (occupation mentioned in A). What difference do you
think it would make in your life?

56/

57/

58/

59/

---

20. A. IF SELF-EMPLOYED: Are most of the people (you/your husband) presently
serve(s) of Japanese ancestry?

Yes 1   60/

No 2

Don't know . 8

B. IF NOT SELF-EMPLOYED: Is (your/your husband's) present employer a
Japanese or Japanese-American individual or concern?

Yes 1   61/

No 2

Don't know . 8

21. We've been talking about (your/your husband's) present (usual) job. Now, I'd like you to tell me about the full-time position (you/he) held just before this one, whether it was a job in the same firm or a change from another firm.

BEGIN DECK 02

OCCUPATION: _____

_____

_____   10-12/

_____

No former job (SKIP TO Q. 23) 0

A. When (you/he) took that job, did it involve a shift in firms, or did (you/he) change duties within the same firm?

Changed firms 1   13/

Same firm 2

First job held 0

Don't know 8

B. About what year did (you/he) start on that job, and when did (you/he) leave it?

_____   _____   14-15/
(year began) to (year ended)

C. Did the change to (your/his) present job from the one we're talking about now involve a change from one firm to another?

Yes 1   16/

No 2

Don't know . . 8

D. Why did (you/he) make that change? (Any other reasons?)   17-18/

19/

ASK Q. 22 A, B, AND C FOR EACH JOB RESPONDENT (R'S HUSBAND) HAS HELD, WORKING BACK
TO HIS FIRST FULL-TIME JOB.

22. And now I'd like you to tell me about all (your/his) other past full-time jobs--
whether or not a change in firm was involved. Let's take this back to (your/
his) first full-time position.

A. What job did (you/he) hold before the one we just talked about?	B. What year did (you/he) take that job?	C. Was that a different firm from the one (you/he) worked for just before that?	SPECIAL CODING
	Year	Same | Different	
1.		S D	
2.		S D	
3.		S D	
4.		S D	
5.		S D	
6.		S D	
7.		S D	
8.		S D	
9.		S D	
10.		S D	
11		S D	
12.		S D	
13.		S D	
14.		S D	
15.		S D	

ASK Q'S. 23 AND 24 ONLY FOR CURRENTLY SELF-EMPLOYED RESPONDENTS (HUSBANDS) WHO RE-
PORT SAME JOB SINCE 1960. INCLUDE FARMERS UNLESS THEY ARE AGRICULTURAL LABORERS.
FOR OTHERS, SKIP TO Q. 25.

23. Since 1960 has the size of your (husband's) (holdings/establishment) increased,
decreased, or remained about the same?

Increased	. 1	20/
Same	 2	
Decreased	. 3	
Don't know	. 8	

24. Since 1960, have your (husband's) earnings from (your/his) (holdings/estab-
lishment) on the whole increased, decreased, or stayed about the same?

Increased	. 1	21/
Same	 2	
Decreased	. 3	
Don't know	. 8	

ASK EVERYONE:

25. About what proportion of the people (you/your husband) see(s) regularly at
work on (your/his) present job are Japanese Americans--nearly all, about
three-quarters, about half, about a quarter, almost none, or none at all?

Meets no one at work	. 0	22/
Nearly all	 1	
About 3/4	 2	
About 1/2	 3	
About 1/4	 4	
Almost none	 5	
None	 6	
Don't know	 8	

26. Now, about the people (you/your husband) see(s) at work--(do you/does he)
meet them off the job often, sometimes, or almost never?

Often	. . . 1	23/
Sometimes	. 2	
Almost never	3	
Don't know	. 8	

ASK Q. 27 ONLY IF <u>CURRENTLY MARRIED</u>; OTHERWISE GO TO Q. 28.

<u>ASK ABOUT RESPONDENT IF FEMALE</u>.
<u>ASK ABOUT WIFE IF R IS MALE</u>.

27. (Does your wife/Do you) work?

                           Yes . . (ASK A) . . . 1   24/

                           No . (GO TO Q. 28) . 2

     A. <u>IF YES</u>: Is that a full-time or a part-time job?

                           Full-time 1   25/

                           Part-time 2

---

28. A. Please give me the letter next to the category on this card which includes your present total family income. HAND RESPONDENT CARD 1. Please include income from rents, investments, interest and earnings of all family members--in other words, the approximate total income as recorded on your last income tax.

     B. And which letter represents what you think your family income will be in five years?

	A. Total Family Income	B. Income in Five Years
A. Under $2,500	1 26/	1 27/
B. $2,500 - $4,999	2	2
C. $5,000 - $7,499	3	3
D. $7,500 - $9,999	4	4
E. $10,000 - $14,999 . . .	5	5
F. $15,000 - $19,999 . . .	6	6
G. $20,000 - $29,999 . . .	7	7
H. $30,000 or more	8	8
Don't know	9	9

Now I have some questions about your education.

29.

	A. What was the highest grade you completed in school?		B. (1) IF YES TO B. Highest grade in Japan?	
Never attended school	0	28/	0	29/
1-4 grades/years	1		1	
5-7 grades/years	2		2	
8 grades/years	3		3	
9-11 grades/years	4		4	
12 grades/years (high school grad.)	5		5	
13-15 years (some college) . . .	6		6	
16 years (completed college) . .	7		7	
More than 16 years (beyond college graduation)	8		8	

ASK B AND C ONLY OF RESPONDENTS WHO HAVE PREVIOUSLY MENTIONED A JAPANESE RESIDENCE.

B.   Did you receive any schooling in Japan?

    IF YES, ASK (1) AND C.

    IF NO, CIRCLE "0" IN COLUMN B. (1) ABOVE.

    (1)   What was the highest level of schooling you completed in Japan? CIRCLE CODE IN COLUMN B.(1) ABOVE.

    (C)   How many years of school did you attend in Japan, altogether?

                         _____   30-31/

---

30.   Did you attend Japanese language school when you were young?

                              Yes 1   32/

                              No 2

                              Don't know . 8

IF EVER MARRIED, ASK Q. 31; OTHERWISE SKIP TO Q. 32.

31.　A.　What was the highest grade your (wife/husband) completed in school?

Never attended school 0	33/
1-4 grades/years 1	
5-7 grades/years 2	
8 grades/years 3	
9-11 grades/years 4	
12 years 5	
13-15 years (some college) . . 6	
16 years (completed college) . 7	
Graduate work 8	
Don't know 9	

　B.　Did (she/he) receive any schooling in Japan?

　　IF YES, ASK (1). IF NO, CIRCLE "0" IN (1) BELOW.

　　(1)　How many years of school did (he/she) attend in Japan, altogether?

　　　　　　　　　　　　　　　　　　_____　34-35/

　　　　　　　　　Received no schooling in Japan . . 0

32.　Did anyone in your or your (spouse's) family ever give (you/your husband) any...

	Yes	No or Don't know	
A. ...advice in choosing a career?	01	00	36-37/
B. ...work for pay, even part-time, in a business or farm owned by members of the family?	02	00	
C. (ASK ONLY OF THOSE WHO HAVE EVER BEEN FARMERS) ...help in acquiring a farm? . . .	04	00	
D. (ASK ONLY OF THOSE WHO HAVE EVER OWNED A BUSINESS) ...help in acquiring a business?	08	00	
E. ...help in getting a job?	16	00	
IF NO TO ALL OF THESE, CIRCLE CODE ————————>	32		

33. Now, would you tell me whether there has been anyone from <u>outside</u> the family
    who has given you (your husband) help in (your/his) advancement--either in
    any of these same ways, or in other ways?

    Yes . (ASK A - E) . . . 1   38/
    No . . (GO TO Q. 34) . . 2
    Don't know (GO TO Q. 34) 8

IF YES:

A. Who (is/was) that? <u>HAND RESPONDENT CARD 2</u>. (Is/Was) his relationship
    to (you/your husband) any one of those on the card? (IF MORE THAN ONE:
    Who is the person who helped you the most?) CIRCLE ONLY ONE CODE.

    Friend of family or of in-laws 001 39-41/
    Teacher or school official 002
    Work superior 004
    Work peer 008
    <u>Genro</u>; community sage 016
    Individual with community influence . . 032
    Political leader 064
    Recruiter from business; talent scout . 128
    Other (SPECIFY) 256
    Don't know 888

B. When was this? About how old (were you/was he)
    when that person <u>first</u> started to help (you/him)?

    _____ years   42-43/

C. Did that person help (you/him) in this   Only once 1   44/
    way (these ways) only once, or did he   A number of times . . . 2
    do so a number of times, or does he   Still helps sometimes . 3
    still continue to help (you/him)   Don't know 8
    sometimes?

D. What kind of help did he give (you/him)? FIELD CODE AND CIRCLE AS MANY
    AS R MENTIONS.

    Advice in choosing a career 01 45-47/
    Work, even part-time 02
    Help in acquiring a farm or business 04
    Help in getting a job 08
    Bring (R's/husband's) work to atten-
      tion of others 16
    Support in school or college 32
    Other (SPECIFY) 64
    Don't know, can't say 88

E. And was this person a Japanese American?

    Yes 1   48/
    No 2
    Don't know . . 8

34. When you were in high school, would you say there was any particular occupation your parents hoped you would enter?

    Yes 1   49/

    No 2

    Don't know . 8

---

35. Parents often try to influence their children when it comes to marriage. Was
this true of your parents in your case?

    Yes . . . . (ASK A) . . . 1   50/

    No . (GO TO Q. 36) . . . 2

    Don't know; don't
    remember 8

    A. IF YES: What did they urge you to do? (What was the situation?)

    51-52/

    53-54/

---

36. How about yourself? (Have you or will you/would you) try to influence your
children when it comes to marriage?

    Yes . . . . (ASK A) . . . 1   55/

    No . (GO TO Q. 37) . . . 2

    Don't know 8

    A. IF YES: What (have/would) you urge them to do?

    56-57/

    58-59/

37. For each of the principles I will now read to you, tell me whether or not
     your parents stressed it when you were growing up.

	Stressed it	Didn't	Don't recall	
A. You must behave properly to avoid bringing shame to the family	1	2	8	60/
B. To lose a competition is to be disgraced	1	2	8	61/
C. One must make returns for all kindnesses received	1	2	8	62/
D. You must act so as not to bring dishonor to the Japanese American community	1	2	8	63/

38.

	A. While you were growing up, would you say that your parents wanted you to take an active part with Caucasians in their activities, or to stick pretty much with Japanese Americans?		B. (Do you) (Would you) want your own children to take an active part with Caucasians in their activities, or to stick pretty much with Japanese Americans?	
Active part with Caucasians . . .	1	64/	1	65/
Stick to Japanese Americans . . .	2		2	
Neither; both; nothing in particular	3		3	
Don't know	8		8	

39. While you were in grade school, were most of your close friends Japanese Americans, non-Japanese, or about an equal number of both?

No friends 0   66/
Mostly Japanese Americans . 1
Equal number 2
Mostly non-Japanese 3
Don't know 8

40. And what about when you were in high school? (Were most of your close friends Japanese Americans, non-Japanese, or about an equal number of both?)

No friends 0   67/
Mostly Japanese Americans . 1
Equal number 2
Mostly non-Japanese 3
Don't know 8

41. Now let's talk about the people who are presently closest friends outside your immediate family--I mean the people whom you see most often or feel closest to.

A. So that I don't mix them up, please tell me the first name of each friend. RECORD NAMES AND ASK B-D FOR FRIEND 1. THEN ASK B-D FOR FRIEND 2.	B. Does (friend) live on the same block as you do, in the same neighborhood, in the same city (county), or further away?				C. Is (he/she) an Issei, a Nisei, a Sansei, a Caucasian, or of another background?				
	Blk.	Nbhd.	City	Further	Is-sei	Ni-sei	San-sei	Cauca-sian	Other (SPEC-IFY)
FRIEND 1:	1	2	3	10/ 4	1	2	3	4	12/ 5
FRIEND 2:	1	2	3	11/ 4	1	2	3	4	13/ 5

D. What is (first friend's) occupation?

OCCUPATION: _____ 14-16/

_____

What is (second friend's) occupation?

OCCUPATION: _____ 17-19/

_____

42. A. About how many groups or organizations do you belong to? I mean groups which have a more or less regular membership and meet more or less regularly. In the count, please don't include the church you belong to; we'll come to that later.

	A. Total number of groups.		B. Number of Japanese American groups.	
None . (GO TO Q. 43)	0	20/	0	21/
One . . (ASK B-D)	1		1	
Two . . (ASK B-D)	2		2	
Three . (ASK B-D)	3		3	
Four-Five (ASK B-D)	4		4	
Six-Nine (ASK B-D)	5		5	
Ten-Twenty-four (ASK B-D) . .	6		6	
Twenty-five or more (ASK B-D).	7		7	
Don't know (GO TO Q. 43) . . .	8		8	

IF BELONGED TO ANY GROUPS:

B. (Does that group have mostly Japanese American members?)
(Of these groups, how many have mostly Japanese American members?)
CODE ABOVE UNDER COLUMN B.

C. Are you now an officer or a committee member of any of the organizations you belong to?

Yes . . . 1   22/

No 2

D. Of all the organizations you belong to, what is the name of the one to which you devote the most time? (IF ACTIVITY OR FUNCTION NOT CLEAR FROM NAME, ASK: Could you tell me what that organization does?)

_____ 23-24/

_____ 25/

43. Suppose (you/your husband) were given an extra one month's salary which you could spend in any way you wanted. How would you spend it?

26-27/

44. In your opinion, which is more often to blame if a person is poor--a lack of
    effort on his own part or circumstances beyond his control?

Lack of own effort	1	28/
Circumstances beyond control .	2	
Both	3	
Don't know	8	

45. Who do you think has higher social value--people who make, buy, or sell
    things of practical use, or people like scholars and artists?

Practical use	1	29/
Scholars and artists .	2	
Don't know	8	

46. If you think a thing is right, do you think you should go ahead and do it
    even if it is contrary to usual custom, or do you think it's better to
    follow custom?

Go ahead	1	30/
Follow custom	2	
Don't know	8	

47. If you did not have any children, do you think you ought to adopt a child
    to continue the family line even if the child were not related to you, or do
    you think you need not do that?

Should adopt	1	31/
Need not adopt	2	
Other (SPECIFY) . . .	3	
Don't know	8	

48.	A. Would you say that generally the Nisei are not American enough, too American, or just about right?		B. And what about the Sansei?	
Not American enough	1	32/	1	33/
Just about right	2		2	
Too American	3		3	
Don't know	8		8	

49. Would you say that in general the Nisei are more like the Issei or more like the Sansei?

> More like Issei (ASK A) . . 1   34/
>
> Equally similar to both . . 2
>
> More like Sansei (ASK A) . . 3
>
> Don't know 8

   A. <u>IF MORE LIKE ISSEI OR SANSEI</u>: In what ways are they more like (Issei/ Sansei) than (Sansei/Issei)?

> 35/
>
> 36/
>
> 37/

---

50. For each of the following statements, I would like you to tell me whether you think it is definitely true, probably true, probably not true, or definitely true.

	Definitely True	Probably True	Probably Not True	Definitely Not **True**	Don't know	
A. In general, the Issei generation worked harder than the Nisei.	1	2	3	4	8	38/
B. In general, the Issei weren't enough concerned about what Caucasians would think of them.	1	2	3	4	8	39/
C. In general, the Nisei were brought up too strictly by the Issei.	1	2	3	4	8	40/
D. In general, the Nisei generation is less willing than the Issei to push ahead with risky ventures.	1	2	3	4	8	41/

51. HAND RESPONDENT SELF-ADMINISTERED QUESTION SECTION.
Here is a page of questions which you can fill out more easily yourself. All we want to know is whether you agree or disagree with each of the statements on the sheet. Please circle an answer code for each question, even if you are not sure of your answer. There are no right or wrong answers. All we want is the answer that comes to your mind first.

TAKE BACK SHEET. Thank you very much. Now I'll ask you some more questions concerning your opinions.

52. HAND RESPONDENT CARD 3. Tell me which item on this list you would want most (for your husband) on a job. Now, would you rank the others in the order of importance to you (for your husband)? (PROBE: Which comes next? Which third? Which fourth? Which fifth? And which last?)

	Ranks first	Ranks 2nd	Ranks 3rd	Ranks 4th	Ranks 5th	Ranks 6th
A. Income is steady	1 42/	1 43/	1 44/	1 45/	1 46/	1 47/
B. Income is high	2	2	2	2	2	2
C. There is no danger of being fired or unemployed	3	3	3	3	3	3
D. Working hours are short, lots of free time . .	4	4	4	4	4	4
E. Chances of getting ahead are good	5	5	5	5	5	5
F. The work is important and gives a feeling of accomplishment	6	6	6	6	6	6
Don't know; no opinion .	8	8	8	8	8	8

IF MARRIED TO JAPANESE AMERICAN, ASK Q. 53; OTHERWISE GO TO Q. 54.

53. How much do you think that being a Japanese American has hindered your (husband's) advancement--not at all, only a little, somewhat, or very much?

Not at all 1   48/
Only a little . . . 2
Somewhat 3
Very much 4
Has helped 5
Don't know 8

54. Of all the Japanese Americans you have known or known about in the communities where you have lived, think of the one person who stands out in your mind as the most important leader. We don't need to know his name, but we do want to know if you know him personally, or if you know of him only by reputation?

Know personally . . . . . (ASK A AND B) . . 1	49/
Know by reputation only . (ASK A AND B) . . 2
Don't know of any leader (SKIP TO Q. 55) . 0

IF KNOWS OF LEADER:

A. In your opinion, why was he a leader?

50/

51/

B. And, as best you can remember, what was his occupation during the prime of his life?

52-53/

55. Now, a few more questions about leadership and the Japanese American people. HAND RESPONDENT CARD 4.

	A. Which one of the five things on this card is **most** important for a Japanese American community leader today, as you see it?		B. And which one do you think is **least** important today?	
A. Gaining concrete improvements for the Japanese American community.	1	54/	1	55/
B. Joining with other groups to make a better America.	2		2	
C. Leading a virtuous life	3		3	
D. Settling disputes and squabbles in the Japanese American community	4		4	
E. Winning the respect of Caucasians	5		5	
Don't know	8		8	

56. During the World War II relocation, some Nisei worked to make relocation as orderly and comfortable as possible, while others protested the injustice of the relocation and tried to have it declared unconstitutional. Which kind of leader do you <u>now</u> think employed the better approach?

Orderly and comfortable 1		56/
Protest 2		
Can't generalize; both; neither . 3		
Don't know 8		

57. Just as during the relocation period there were differences among Japanese Americans about how to act, we've heard that nowadays there are differences of opinion about how to handle important issues facing the group. Do you yourself believe that such differences exist now?

Yes (ASK A) . . 1   57/
No (GO TO Q. 58) 2
Don't know . . 8

A. <u>IF YES</u>: What are these differences of opinion about? (PROBE.)

58/

59/

58. A. Do you suppose that most Caucasians in America would be disturbed if...

	Yes	No	Don't know	
...a Japanese American girl married a son of theirs? . .	1	2	8	60/
...a Japanese American boy married a daughter of theirs?.	1	2	8	61/

B. And do you suppose that <u>you</u> would be disturbed if...

...a son of yours married a Caucasian girl?	1	2	8	62/
...a daughter of yours married a Caucasian boy?	1	2	8	63/

59. As I read some ways in which discrimination against the Japanese Americans is said to have occurred, will you please tell me, for each one, whether or not in the past ten years or so you or your immediate family... ASK A AND THEN EITHER B OR C FOR EACH ITEM (1) THROUGH (4).

FOR EACH NO TO A, ASK B.   FOR EACH YES TO A, ASK C.   BEGIN DECK 04

	A. ...have experienced it personally?			B. IF NO TO A: Have you heard about cases in which other Japanese Americans experienced it within the past ten years?			C. IF YES TO A: Were you taken by surprise when you experienced (discrimination)?		
	Yes (ASK C)	No (ASK B)	Don't know	Yes	No	Don't know	Sur-prised	Not sur-prised	Don't know
1) Discrimination in housing?	1	0	8	2	0	8	10/	1	2	8	11/
2) Discrimination in schools?	1	0	8	2	0	8	12/	1	2	8	13/
3) Discrimination in jobs?	1	0	8	2	0	8	14/	1	2	8	15/
4) Police brutality?	1	0	8	2	0	8	16/	1	2	8	17/

60. Members of many minority groups in America have complained that their groups are not being treated as full and equal Americans. Which of the groups I will read to you can rightfully complain that they are not being treated as full and equal Americans today?

	Can rightfully complain	Cannot	Don't know	
A. Negroes?	1	2	8	18/
B. Italian Americans? . .	1	2	8	19/
C. Japanese Americans? .	1	2	8	20/
D. Chinese Americans? . .	1	2	8	21/
E. Jews?	1	2	8	22/
F. Mexican Americans? . .	1	2	8	23/
G. Puerto Ricans?	1	2	8	24/

61. A. Negroes are interested in bettering their position in American society.
         What advice would you give Negroes, as a race, to achieve their goals?

                                                                                      25/

                                                                                      26/

                                                                                      27/

     B. How long do you think it will take for the Negroes to achieve their
         goals? DO NOT READ CATEGORIES. CIRCLE ONLY ONE CODE.

         They've already achieved them . . . . (GO TO Q. 62) 0   28/
         Less than a year; "a very short time" (GO TO Q. 62) 1
         1 to less than 5 years; "a few years" . . . (ASK C) 2
         5-9 years . . . . (ASK C) . . . 3
         10-24 years . . . . (ASK C) . . . 4
         25-49 years "a generation" . . . . (ASK C) . . . 5
         50-99 years "two generations"; "a couple of generations" (ASK C) . 6
         100 years or more . . . . (ASK C) . . . 7
         Never . . . . (GO TO Q. 62) 8
         Don't know; can't say . . . . (GO TO Q. 62) 9

     C. IF 1-100 YEARS: What will keep them from achieving their goals
         sooner? (PROBE: What else?)

                                                                                      29/

                                                                                      30/

                                                                                      31/

Now I'd like to find out something about your religious affiliations.

62. Are you a Buddhist, a Protestant,
a Roman Catholic, a nonbeliever,
or something else?

Nonbeliever 1 32/
Buddhist 2
Protestant 3
Roman Catholic 4
Konko Kyo (Shinto) . . . 5
Ba'hai; World Messianity;
  Seicho-No-Ie 6
Other (SPECIFY) 7

---

63. Have you at an earlier time been a member
of a (different) religion?

Yes . . . (ASK A) 1 33/
No . . (GO TO Q. 64) . . 2

  A. **IF YES**: What religion was that?
    (IF MORE THAN ONE, RECORD <u>FIRST</u>
    BELONGED TO.)

Nonbeliever 1 34/
Buddhist 2
Protestant 3
Roman Catholic 4
Konko Kyo (Shinto) . . . 5
Ba'hai; World Messianity;
  Seicho-No-Ie 6
Other (SPECIFY) 7

> IF RESPONDENT NOW BUDDHIST, HAND HIM CARD 5 AND ASK Q. 64 A.
> IF RESPONDENT NOW PROTESTANT, ASK Q. 64 B.

64. A. You said you now are a Buddhist.
    Which of these sects are you a
    member of?

(1) Jodo Shinshu (Nishi   35-
    Hongwanji) 41 36/
(2) Jodo Shinshu (Higashi
    Hongwanji) 42
(3) Jodo Shu 43
(4) Nichiren Shu 44
(5) Zen 45
(6) Shingon Shu (Koyasan) . 46
(7) Other 47

  B. You said you are a Protestant.
    What denomination do you belong
    to?

Methodist 02
Presbyterian 03
Episcopal 04
Seventh Day Adventist . . . 05
Churches of Christ 06
Congregationalist 07
Holiness 08
Lutheran 09
Mormon 10
United Church of Christ . . 11
Baptist 12
Other (SPECIFY) 17
None 77

<u>IF CLERGYMAN, CODE Q. 65 WITHOUT ASKING.</u>

65. How often do you usually attend religious services--once a week, a few times a month, once a month, or less often than that?

Once a week or more . . 1	37/
Few times a month . . . 2	
Once a month 3	
Less often than that . . 4	
Never 5	
Don't know; can't say . 8	

<u>ASK EVERYONE</u>:

66. Aside from attendance at religious services, how important would you say religion is to you--very important, fairly important, or not important at all?

Very important 1	38/
Fairly important 2	
Not important at all . . 3	
Don't know; can't say . 8	

67. What religion does your (wife/husband) belong to? Is (she/he) a Buddhist, a Protestant, a Roman Catholic, a non-believer, or something else?

Nonbeliever 1	39/
Buddhist 2	
Protestant 3	
Roman Catholic 4	
Konko Kyo (Shinto) . . . 5	
Ba'hai; World Messianity; Seicho-No-Ie 6	
Other (SPECIFY) 7	
Don't know 8	

Just a few more questions about yourself now.

68. Which political party do you generally support in national elections?

Democratic 1	40/
Republican 2	
Independent 3	
Other (SPECIFY) 4	
Don't vote 8	

69. Generally speaking, how much interest would you say you have in politics-- a great deal, a fair amount, only a little, or no interest at all?

A great deal 1	41/
A fair amount 2	
Only a little 3	
No interest at all . . . 4	

70. During the last few months, has anyone outside your family asked you for
advice about politics or public affairs?

Yes . . . . 1　42/
No 2
Don't know . 8

71. What magazines do you subscribe to or regularly read?　(Any others?)

None . . . 000

1. _____　　6. _____　43/
2. _____　　7. _____
3. _____　　8. _____　44/
4. _____　　9. _____
5. _____　　10. _____　45/

72. Do you ever read any Japanese American newspapers?　Yes . (ASK A) . 1　46/
No (GO TO Q. 73) 2

A. Do you read them regularly, occasionally, or hardly ever?

Regularly . . . 1　47/
Occasionally . . 2
Hardly ever . . 3

ASK EVERYONE:

73. Are you able to speak Japanese quite fluently, pretty well, only a little, or
not at all?

Quite fluently . . . 1　48/
Pretty well 2
Only a little 3
Not at all 4

74. Are you able to read Japanese?

Yes . . . . 1　49/
No 2

75. IF HAS CHILDREN: Do you think your children
ought to know how to speak Japanese?

Yes . . . . . . 1　50/

IF HAS NO CHILDREN: If you had children,
do you think they ought to know how to
speak Japanese?

No 2

Not certain . . 8

76. Have you ever visited Japan [aside from the time(s) you lived there]?

Yes 1	51/
No 2	

77. Have you (or your wife/husband) ever been a member of a labor union?

Yes 1	52/
No 2	
Don't know . 8	

78. IF EVER MARRIED: (Have you/Has your husband) ever served in the United States armed forces, active or reserve?

Yes . . . (ASK A) . . . 1	53/
No . . (GO TO Q. 79) . . 2	
Don't know (GO TO Q. 79) 8	

    A. IF YES: In what year did (you/your husband) first enter the service?

Before 1941 . . 1	54/
1941-1945 . . . 2	
1946-1949 . . . 3	
1950-1953 . . . 4	
1954-1963 . . . 5	
1964-present . . 6	
Don't know . . . 8	

79. IF EVER MARRIED AND HAS CHILDREN, HAND RESPONDENT SANSEI LISTING SHEET.

As you know, we are doing a study of three generations of Japanese American families--the Issei, the Nisei, and the Sansei. We will need, therefore, information about your children. Here is a sheet for you to fill out. Would you please enter the name, sex, age, and address of all your children, whether or not living at home? Also please enter whether each of your children is of this or a previous marriage, and whether he is natural or adopted. You only have to enter the family name where it is different from yours; and it will be sufficient, for those children living with you in the home, simply to enter "at home."

SAY TO EVERYONE:

Thank you very much for your time and cooperation. You have been an invaluable help. And I hope you have enjoyed the interview.

ENTER HERE   [_____ AM / PM]   TIME INTERVIEW ENDED.   55/

IMMEDIATELY UPON COMPLETING INTERVIEW FILL OUT ITEMS A AND B.

A. TYPE OF INTERVIEW: Face to face . . 1   56/
                                         Telephone . . . 2

B. SEX OF RESPONDENT: Male 1   57/
                                         Female 2

FILL OUT THE FOLLOWING ITEMS, C - M, AS SOON AS POSSIBLE AFTER COMPLET-ING THE INTERVIEW, SO THAT IT IS STILL FRESH IN YOUR MIND.

C. DWELLING TYPE: Unknown: telephone interview . 0   58/
                        Single family 1
                        Two family 2
                        Multiple dwelling:
                          1 - 9 units 3
                          10 - 24 units 4
                          25 or more units 5
                        Rooming house 6
                        Hotel 7
                        Other (SPECIFY) 8

D. FLUENCY IN ENGLISH: Perfect 1   59/
                                         Nearly perfect . . 2
                                         Some difficulty . 3
                                         Much difficulty . 4

E. COOPERATIVENESS:
                        Very cooperative 1   60/
                        Fairly cooperative . . . 2
                        Uncooperative 3

F. INTEREST:
                        Great interest . . 1   61/
                        Some interest . . 2
                        Little interest . 3

G. RECORD RELATIONSHIP TO RESPONDENT OF ANYONE ELSE PRESENT DURING
    INTERVIEW OTHER THAN RESPONDENT AND INTERVIEWER.

                                                              62/

H. NOTE ANY INTERRUPTIONS IN, DISTURBANCES DURING, OR PECULIAR CIRCUM-
    STANCES OF, THE INTERVIEW.

                                                              63/

I. NOTE ANY QUESTIONS THE RESPONDENT SEEMED TO HAVE PARTICULAR DIFFI-
    CULTY UNDERSTANDING.

J. Do you think it made any difference in   Yes (ANSWER K) . 1   64/
    the responses you got that you were not
    a Japanese American?   No 2

K. How did it make a difference? On what questions and to what extent?

L. Date interview completed: | | | | 6 | 7 | 65/
                                  Month Date Year

M. Your signature: _____ 66-68/

Thank you for your cooperation!   PSU NO: | | | |
                                                   69 70 71

Appendix B:
Sansei Interview Schedule

FAMILY IDs

☐☐☐☐☐☐☐☐☐

JAPANESE AMERICAN RESEARCH PROJECT

University of California at Los Angeles

YOUR NAME: _____

NUMBER AND STREET: _____

CITY AND STATE: _____

DATE YOU FILLED OUT THIS
QUESTIONNAIRE: _____

This survey is supported by a grant
from the U.S. Public Health Service.
The directors of the study assume
full responsibility for the contents
of this questionnaire.

TO OUR RESPONDENT:

Most of the questions we are asking you to answer in this questionnaire ask you for *facts* about yourself or others you know: please answer each of these to the best of your ability. We appreciate accuracy, but it will not be necessary for you anywhere on this questionnaire to refer to your records. Just use your memory as best you can. Some other questions ask for your *opinions*. On these questions, obviously, there are no right or wrong answers. What we want to know is *just what you think*. When you aren't quite certain what your answer should be, please give us the choice that appeals to you more at the moment. Please record any additional comments you may have about particular questions or the questionnaire as a whole. Such comments are often invaluable in interpreting your answers to other questions.

None of the questions should be hard or tricky; you will find most are both short and easy. Please remember that it is *you* we are trying to find out about. It will be best, therefore, if you fill out the entire questionnaire *before* you discuss any of the questions with anyone else. After you are finished with the questionnaire, please feel free to discuss it; but be sure you promptly return the filled-out questionnaire to us in the envelope provided.

Instructions for answering each question are printed in CAPITALS along with the question. You are asked to record your answers in one of three ways for any given question. Please always record your answers as neatly as possible.

(1) Most questions require you only to place
a *check* in the box representing the answer.

Yes . . . . . ☑

No . . . . . ☐

(2) Some questions ask you to *fill in* an
appropriate number, word, or phrase on a
line.

23 years

(3) A few questions ask you to *write your
answer out freely* in a large space provided.

Some questions are to be answered by some but not all people. Explanations are provided in every case, sometimes with arrows drawn in to assist you.

You may wonder about the numbers in the right-hand column on each page and near the checkboxes. These numbers are there to aid us in tabulating your responses statistically.

THANK YOU VERY MUCH. WE HOPE YOU ENJOY THE QUESTIONNAIRE, AND WE LOOK FORWARD EAGERLY TO RECEIVING YOUR ANSWERS.

1. What is your sex? **(CHECK ONE)**

Male .... ☐¹   *11*

Female .... ☐²

2. How old were you on your last birthday? **(FILL IN NUMBER BELOW)**

_____ years   *12-13*

3. Where were you born? **(FILL IN BELOW)**

_____ , _____   *14-16*
      (City)   (State)

4. Are you single, married, divorced, separated, or widowed? **(CHECK ONE)**

Single .... ☐¹   *17*

Married .... ☐²

Divorced .... ☐³

Separated .... ☐⁴

Widowed .... ☐⁵

IF YOU WERE EVER MARRIED, ANSWER QUESTIONS 5 AND 6. OTHERWISE ANSWER QUESTION 7.

5A. Where was your spouse born? **(FILL IN BELOW)**

_____ , _____   *18-20*
      (City)   (State)

5B. What is your spouse's background? Is (he/she) a Nisei, a Sansei, a Yonsei, a Caucasian, or of some other background? **(CHECK ONE)**

Nisei .... ☐¹   *21*

Sansei .... ☐²

Yonsei .... ☐³

Caucasian .... ☐⁴

Other background **(PLEASE SPECIFY AT LEFT)** .... ☐⁵

6. How many children have been born to you and your spouse, not counting stillbirths? **(FILL IN NUMBER OF BOYS AND GIRLS BELOW; ENTER "0" WHEN NONE)**

_____ boys   _____ girls   *22*
     23

A. **(IF YOU HAVE HAD ANY CHILDREN)** How old is your oldest child? **(FILL IN BELOW)**

_____ years   *24-25*

IF YOU HAVE *NEVER* BEEN MARRIED, ANSWER QUESTION 7. OTHERWISE SKIP TO QUESTION 8.

7. Are you currently engaged, going steady with one person, dating casually, or not dating at all?
   (CHECK ONE)

          Engaged **(ANSWER A)** . . . . ☐¹   26

          Going steady **(ANSWER A)** . . . . ☐²

          Dating casually **(GO TO QUESTION 8)**. . ☐³

          Not dating **(GO TO QUESTION 8)** . . . . . ☐⁴

➤ A. Is the person you are engaged to or go steady with a Nisei, a Sansei, a Yonsei, a Caucasian,
   or of some other background? **(CHECK ONE)**

          Nisei . . . . ☐¹   27

          Sansei . . . . ☐²

          Yonsei . . . . ☐³

          Caucasian . . . . ☐⁴

          Other background **(PLEASE SPECIFY AT
          LEFT)** . . . . ☐⁵

EVERYBODY ANSWER:

8. What do you think is the ideal number of children for a married couple to have in America today?   28
   (FILL IN NUMBER BELOW)

                    _____ children

9. Do your own parents live in the same household as you do, or do they live somewhere else in the same
   neighborhood, or somewhere else in the same metropolitan area or county as yourself, or do they live
   farther away than that? **(CHECK ONE)**

          Same household . . . . ☐¹   29

          Same neighborhood . . . . . ☐²

          Same metropolitan area
            or county . . . . ☐³

          Farther away . . . . ☐⁴

10. Aside from your parents and your own spouse and children, about how many other relatives –
    including *anyone* else you *consider* a relative – live in the same metropolitan area or county as
    yourself? **(IF ANY)** And about how many live in the same neighborhood as yourself? **(IF ANY)** And
    how many of these live in the same household as you? **(FILL IN TABLE BELOW)**

	In metro area or county	In neighborhood	In household
Number of relatives	_____	_____	_____

    30-31

    32-33

    34-35

THOSE WITH RELATIVES LIVING IN THE SAME METROPOLITAN AREA OR COUNTY, ANSWER QUESTION 11. OTHERS SKIP TO QUESTION 12.

11. About how many times in the past month have you visited with or been visited by relatives living in the same neighborhood or metropolitan area or county as you? Please do *not include* visits from any relatives who live in the same household as you. **(FILL IN NUMBER BELOW)**

_____ times   36-37

EVERYBODY ANSWER:

12. Now we want to find out about the various *cities and towns* you have lived in. For the metropolitan area or county you *now* live in (line 1, below), please fill in the date you moved there. Then please go back, step by step, to your birth place, answering for each metropolitan area or county you have lived in, questions **A, B,** and **C. (FILL IN TABLE BELOW)**

A. Name of each city or town, and state each is located in. **(FILL IN BELOW; LINE 1 REPRESENTS THE METROPOLITAN AREA OR COUNTY YOU NOW LIVE IN)**	B. In what year did you move to each? **(APPROXIMATE DATES IF YOU CAN'T REMEMBER EXACTLY)**	C. Were your neighbors there mostly Japanese Americans, mostly non-Japanese Americans, or was the neighborhood mixed? **(CHECK ONE FOR EACH)**			SPEC COD
		Mostly Japanese Americans	Mostly non-Japanese Americans	Mixed	
1. Metropolitan area or county you live in *now.*		☐	☐	☐	
2.		☐	☐	☐	
3.		☐	☐	☐	
4.		☐	☐	☐	
5.		☐	☐	☐	
6.		☐	☐	☐	
7.		☐	☐	☐	
8.		☐	☐	☐	
9.		☐	☐	☐	
10.		☐	☐	☐	

13. Now about the neighborhood you live in now: do you think of this neighborhood as your real home – the place where you really belong, or do you think of it as just a place where you happen to be living? **(CHECK ONE)**

Really belong .... ☐¹

Just a place .... ☐²

38

14A. Would you say that this neighborhood is made up mostly of Japanese Americans, mostly non-Japanese Americans, or is it mixed? **(CHECK ONE)**

Mostly Japanese Americans .... ☐¹

Mixed .... ☐²

Mostly non-Japanese Americans .... ☐³

39

14B. What other kinds of groups besides Japanese Americans live in this neighborhood? **(ANSWER BELOW)**

40-41

Now we want to find out some things about your career to date and about your plans for your career.

15A. What occupation would you *most like* to make your life work – the work you hope to be doing throughout your career? **(DESCRIBE THE OCCUPATION BELOW; PLEASE BE AS SPECIFIC AS YOU CAN AND TELL A LITTLE ABOUT THE DUTIES THIS OCCUPATION ACTUALLY INVOLVES)**

42-44

15B. In this occupation, do you expect you would be working for yourself all the time, working for someone else all the time, or sometimes working for yourself and sometimes for someone else? **(CHECK ONE BELOW)**

Working for yourself .... ☐¹

Sometimes for yourself, sometimes
   for someone else .... ☐²

Working for someone else .... ☐³

45

16. How likely do you think it is that you will *actually* be doing that work, say in ten or twenty years? Do you think it is almost certain, pretty likely, about fifty-fifty, pretty unlikely, or highly unlikely that you will be doing that? **(CHECK ONE BELOW)**

Almost certain **(SKIP TO QUESTION 17)** . . ☐¹   46

Pretty likely **(SKIP TO QUESTION 17)** . . . . ☐²

About fifty-fifty **(ANSWER A AND B)** . . . . . ☐³

Pretty unlikely **(ANSWER A AND B)** . . . . . ☐⁴

Highly unlikely **(ANSWER A AND B)** . . . . . ☐⁵

A. For what reason or reasons do you think that in ten or twenty years you might *not* be in the occupation you would most *like* to be in? **(CHECK ALL REASONS BELOW YOU THINK MAY APPLY)**

Insufficient education . . . . ☐001   47-49

Insufficient skills or talent . . . . ☐002

Occupation too competitive . . . . ☐004

Racial discrimination . . . . ☐008

You need pull . . . . ☐016

You lack drive or ambition . . . . ☐032

You would have to move to take the job . . . . ☐064

Family demands would be too great . . . . . ☐128

Others **(PLEASE DESCRIBE IN SPACE TO LEFT)** . . . . ☐256

B. What other work do you think you actually *will* be doing in ten or twenty years, if you are not in the occupation you think you would most *like* to be in? **(DESCRIBE THE OCCUPATION BELOW: PLEASE BE AS SPECIFIC AS YOU CAN AND TELL A LITTLE ABOUT THE DUTIES THIS OCCUPATION ACTUALLY INVOLVES)**

    50-52

17. Many people feel that they must achieve a certain standing within their occupation before they can call their career a success. Speaking just for yourself now, how high a standing do you hope you will achieve in the life work you think you actually will have? **(CHECK ONE)**

One of the top people in the occupation . . . ☐¹   53

Near the top of the occupation . . . . ☐²

Above average . . . . ☐³

Just about average . . . . ☐⁴

Any secure standing . . . . ☐⁵

Standing makes no difference to me . . . . . ☐⁶

WOMEN **WHO ARE CURRENTLY MARRIED OR WIDOWED: IF YOUR HUSBAND HAS EVER HAD A FULL-TIME JOB (APART FROM VACATION EMPLOYMENT), PLEASE ANSWER QUESTIONS 18 THROUGH 22 IN TERMS OF YOUR** *HUSBAND'S* **OCCUPATIONS; IF YOUR HUSBAND HAS NEVER HAD A FULL-TIME JOB, AND IS STILL A STUDENT, SIMPLY ENTER "STUDENT" FOR QUESTION 18 AND SKIP TO QUESTION 23. WOMEN CURRENTLY SINGLE OR DIVORCED, PLEASE ANSWER QUESTIONS 18 THROUGH 22 IN TERMS OF** *YOUR OWN* **OCCUPATIONS.**

MEN **PLEASE ANSWER QUESTIONS 18 THROUGH 22 IN TERMS OF** *YOUR OWN* **OCCUPATIONS. IF YOU ARE CURRENTLY A STUDENT AND HAVE NEVER HAD A FULL-TIME JOB (APART FROM VACATION EMPLOYMENT), SIMPLY ENTER "STUDENT" IN QUESTION 18 AND SKIP TO QUESTION 23.**

18A.   What kind of work do you or did you do most recently?   **(MARRIED WOMEN:** What kind of work does your husband do or did he do most recently?)   Please be as specific as possible, and tell us briefly what duties the job actually involves and which industry it is part of.   **(ANSWER BELOW)**   54-56

18B.   (Are you/is your husband) self-employed or employed by someone else?   **(CHECK ONE)**

Self-employed . . . . ☐¹   57

Employed by others . . . . . . ☐²

19.   During what years (have you held/has your husband held) this job?   **(FILL IN BELOW. IF (YOU/YOUR HUSBAND)** *CURRENTLY* **HOLDS THIS JOB PLEASE WRITE "NOW" FOR YEAR JOB ENDED.)**   58-59

_____ to _____   60-61
(Year job began)   (Year job ended)

THOSE WHO(SE HUSBANDS) ARE *CURRENTLY* **WORKING, ANSWER QUESTIONS 20 AND 21. OTHERS SKIP TO QUESTION 22.**

20.   About what proportion of the people (you see/your husband sees) regularly at work on (your/his) present job are Japanese Americans – nearly all, about three-quarters, about half, about a quarter, almost none, or none at all?   **(CHECK ONE)**

Nearly all . . . . ☐¹   62

About ¾ . . . . ☐²

About ½ . . . . ☐³

About ¼ . . . . ☐⁴

Almost none . . . . ☐⁵

None . . . . ☐⁶

21. Now, about these people (you see/your husband sees) regularly at work – how often (do you/does he) meet them off the job? Often, sometimes, or almost never? **(CHECK ONE)**

Often . . . . ☐¹   63

Sometimes . . . . ☐²

Almost never . . . . ☐³

22. We already know about your (husband's) most recent job. Now we would like to know about all the *other full-time* jobs (you have/he has) ever held, whether or not these represented changes from one firm to another. Please go back step by step to (your/his) first full-time position, answering for *each* job questions A, B, C, and D. **(FILL IN TABLE BELOW: BE SURE TO INCLUDE CHANGES OF POSITION WITHIN THE SAME FIRM.)**

A. Name of each job and brief description of duties.	B. Year the job began? (Approximate date if you can't remember exactly)	C. About how many employees worked for this firm?	D. Was this a different firm from the one (you/he) worked for just before that? **(CHECK ONE FOR EACH JOB)**		SPEC COD
	Year	Number	Same	Different	
1.			☐	☐	
2.			☐	☐	
3.			☐	☐	
4.			☐	☐	
5.			☐	☐	
6.			☐	☐	
7.			☐	☐	
8.			☐	☐	

IF YOU ARE CURRENTLY MARRIED, PLEASE ANSWER QUESTION 23. OTHERWISE, SKIP TO QUESTION 24.

23. Does the woman of the household work full-time, part-time, or does she not work at all?

Works full-time . . . . ☐¹   64

Works part-time . . . . ☐²

Does not work . . . . ☐³

EVERYBODY ANSWER:

24. A. Please check the box to the right of the range below which includes your own *present* total family income. Please include income from rents, investments, interest and earnings of all family members – in other words, the approximate total income as recorded on your last income tax. Please *do not* include *your parents'* income. **(CHECK ONE IN COLUMN A, BELOW)**

    B. And please check the box that represents what you think your family income will be in five years? **(CHECK ONE IN COLUMN B, BELOW)**

    C. Finally, please check the box that represents what you think your family income will be when (you are/your husband is) at the peak of (your/his) career? **(CHECK ONE IN COLUMN C, BELOW)**

	A. Total Family Income	B. Income in Five Years	C. Peak of Career	
Under $2,500	☐¹	☐¹	☐¹	65
$2,500 – $4,999	☐²	☐²	☐²	
$5,000 – $7,499	☐³	☐³	☐³	
$7,500 – $9,999	☐⁴	☐⁴	☐⁴	
$10,000 – $14,999	☐⁵	☐⁵	☐⁵	66
$15,000 – $19,999	☐⁶	☐⁶	☐⁶	
$20,000 – $29,999	☐⁷	☐⁷	☐⁷	
$30,000 or more	☐⁸	☐⁸	☐⁸	67

25. Are you *now* a student, not presently a student but planning to enter school at a later date, or are you all finished with your schooling? **(CHECK ONE)**   **DECK 02**

Now a student . . . . ☐¹   11
Planning to re-enter school . . . . ☐²
All finished with schooling . . . . ☐³

26A. What is the highest grade you have completed so far in school? **(CHECK ONE. IF YOU HAVE EVER BEEN MARRIED, ALSO ANSWER 26B.)**

26B. What is the highest grade your spouse has completed in school? **(CHECK ONE)**

	A. Your own education	B. Your spouse's education	
Less than high school graduate	☐¹	☐¹	12
12 grades (completed high school)	☐²	☐²	13
13-15 grades or years (trade or technical school or some college) . . .	☐³	☐³	
16 grades or years (completed college)	☐⁴	☐⁴	
More than 16 years (beyond college graduation)	☐⁵	☐⁵	

IF YOU HAVE GONE BEYOND HIGH SCHOOL, ANSWER QUESTIONS 27 AND 28; OTHERWISE SKIP TO QUESTION 29.

27. Please list below any colleges and professional or graduate schools you have attended, their location, the years during which you attended each, the major field or fields you studied, and any degrees attained in each. **(FILL IN TABLE BELOW)**

Name of School	Location	Attended From	To	Major Field(s)	Degree(s) Received	
1.						*14-18*
2.						*19-23*
3.						*24-28*
4.						*29-33*

28. Please tell us a little about the various organizations or groups to which you may have belonged during your college career. For each of the types of groups mentioned below, please answer questions A, B, and C. **(FILL IN TABLE BELOW)**

	A. How many organizations of this type did you belong to?	B. Of these, how many had primarily Japanese American members?	C. How many of this type did you hold office or committee membership in?	
Political or student government organizations, and service groups	_____	_____	_____	*34-36*
Fraternities or sororities	_____	_____	_____	*37-39*
Informal circles or unorganized groups	_____	_____	_____	*40-42*
Other groups (for example recreational, athletic, or hobby groups)	_____	_____	_____	*43-45*

29. Over your entire *high-school* career, about how many clubs, fraternities, and other organizations did you belong to? **(FILL IN APPROXIMATE FIGURE BELOW: IF NONE, ENTER "0")**

_____ organizations   *46*

30. And of all these high school groups, in how many did you hold an office? **(FILL IN APPROXIMATE NUMBER BELOW; IF NONE, ENTER "0")**

_____ organizations   *47*

31. While you were in high school, were most of your close friends Japanese Americans, non-Japanese Americans, or about an equal number of both? **(CHECK ONE)**

Mostly Japanese Americans	☐¹	*48*
An equal number of both	☐²	
Mostly non-Japanese Americans	☐³	

32. And what about when you were back in grade school? Were most of your close friends Japanese Americans, non-Japanese Americans, or about an equal number of both? **(CHECK ONE)**

Mostly Japanese Americans	☐¹	*49*
An equal number of both	☐²	
Mostly non-Japanese Americans	☐³	

33. When you were in high school, was there any particular occupation your parents hoped you would enter? **(CHECK ONE)**   **DECK 03**

Yes **(ANSWER A AND B)**	☐¹	*11*
No.	☐²	

→ A. What was this occupation? **(DESCRIBE AS FULLY AS POSSIBLE BELOW)**   *12-14*

→ B. How much emphasis did your parents place upon your entering this occupation? Would you say that they placed a great deal of emphasis upon it, some emphasis, only a little emphasis, or no emphasis at all? **(CHECK ONE)**

A great deal of emphasis	☐¹	*15*
Some emphasis	☐²	
Only a little emphasis	☐³	
No emphasis at all	☐⁴	

34. While you were growing up, would you say that your parents wanted you to take an active part with Caucasians in their activities, or to stick pretty much with Japanese Americans? **(CHECK ONE)**

Take an active part with Caucasians . . .	☐¹	*16*
Stick pretty much with Japanese Americans	☐²	

35. Would *you* want *your own children* to take an active part with Caucasians in their activities, or to stick pretty much with Japanese Americans? **(CHECK ONE)**

Take an active part with Caucasians . . .	☐¹	*17*
Stick pretty much with Japanese Americans	☐²	

36. For each of the principles listed below (**A** to **D**), please tell us whether or not *your parents* stressed it when you were growing up. **(CHECK THE APPROPRIATE NUMBER TO THE RIGHT OF EACH PRINCIPLE BELOW.)**

	Your parents stressed it	Your parents did not stress it	You don't recall	
A. You must behave properly to avoid bringing shame to the family.	☐¹	☐²	☐⁸	18
B. To lose a competition is to be disgraced.	☐¹	☐²	☐⁸	19
C. One must make returns for all kindnesses received.	☐¹	☐²	☐⁸	20
D. You must act so as not to bring dishonor to the Japanese American community.	☐¹	☐²	☐⁸	21

37. Parents often try to influence their children when it comes to marriage. Has this been true of your parents in your case? **(CHECK ONE)**

Yes . . . . ☐¹   22

No **(GO TO QUESTION 38)** . ☐²

IF YES, PLEASE ANSWER: A. What have they urged you to do? **(ANSWER BELOW)**

23-24

25-26

MEN AND UNMARRIED WOMEN: QUESTIONS 38 AND 39 ASK ABOUT YOUR *OWN* CAREER.
MARRIED WOMEN: QUESTIONS 38 AND 39 ASK ABOUT YOUR *HUSBAND'S* CAREER.

38. Here is a list (A to E) of some types of aid families can give. For each one, we would like to know whether (you/your husband) received such aid from any one in your family or in your spouse's family. **(CHECK THE APPROPRIATE BOX FOR *EACH* FORM OF AID)**

	Received such aid from family or spouse's family	Did not receive such aid, or do not remember	
A. Advice in choosing a career	☐⁰¹	☐⁰⁰	27-28
B. Work for pay, even part-time, in a business or farm owned by members of the family . . .	☐⁰²	☐⁰⁰	
C. Help in acquiring a farm	☐⁰⁴	☐⁰⁰	
D. Help in acquiring a business	☐⁰⁸	☐⁰⁰	
E. Help in getting a job	☐¹⁶	☐⁰⁰	

39. Now, would you tell us whether there has been anyone from *outside* the family who has given (you/your husband) help in advancement — either in any of these same ways, or in other ways? **(CHECK ONE)**

Yes . . . . ☐¹   29

No **(GO TO QUESTION 40)** . ☐²

▶ **IF YES, PLEASE ANSWER:**   A. What was this person's relationship to (you/your husband)?   30-32
We would like to know how this person knew (you/him) and
what was his position that he was able to give help.
(ANSWER BELOW)

▶ **AND PLEASE ANSWER:**   B. When was this? About how old (were you/was your husband)   33-34
when that person *first* started to help? **(FILL IN BELOW)**

_____ years

▶ **AND PLEASE ANSWER:**   C. Did that person help (you/him) in this way only once, or did he
do so a number of times, or does he still continue to help some-
times? **(CHECK ONE)**

Only once . . . . ☐¹   35

A number of times . . . . . . ☐²

Still helps sometimes . . . . ☐³

▶ **AND PLEASE ANSWER:**   D. What kind of help did he give? **(ANSWER BELOW)**

36-38

▶ **AND PLEASE ANSWER:**   E. And was this person a Japanese American? **(CHECK ONE)**

Yes . . . . ☐¹   39

No . . . . ☐²

40. Think for a moment of the grandparent you have known the best. Would you say that you yourself have had very close relations with him or her, rather close relations, not very close, or rather distant relations? **(CHECK ONE)**

Very close relations . . . . ☐¹

Rather close relations . . . . ☐²

Not very close relations . . . . ☐³

Rather distant relations . . . . ☐⁴

40

41. Was the grandparent you have known the best born in Japan? **(CHECK ONE)**

Yes **(ANSWER A)** . . . . ☐¹

No **(SKIP TO QUESTION 42)** ☐²

41

A. Do you know, without looking it up, the prefecture in Japan from which he or she came? **(CHECK ONE)**

Yes . . . . ☐¹

No . . . . ☐²

42

EVERYBODY ANSWER:

42. How familiar would you say you are with the experiences your Japanese grandparents had in getting settled in the United States? Would you say you are very familiar, somewhat familiar, or mainly unfamiliar? **(CHECK ONE)**

Very familiar . . . . ☐¹

Somewhat familiar . . . . ☐²

Mainly unfamiliar . . . . ☐³

43

43. In question 36 we asked you about some principles your parents may have stressed. Now would you, for each of these principles, tell us whether or not *any* of your *Japanese grandparents* stressed it when you were growing up. **(CHECK THE APPROPRIATE BOX TO THE RIGHT OF EACH PRINCIPLE BELOW.)**

	Your grandparents stressed it	Your grandparents did not stress it	You don't recall	
A. You must behave properly to avoid bringing shame to the family.	☐¹	☐²	☐⁸	44
B. To lose a competition is to be disgraced.	☐¹	☐²	☐⁸	45
C. One must make returns for all kindnesses received.	☐¹	☐²	☐⁸	46
D. You must act so as not to bring dishonor to the Japanese American community.	☐¹	☐²	☐⁸	47

44. Would you say that *in general* the Nisei are more like the Issei or more like the Sansei? **(CHECK ONE)**

        More like Issei . . . . ☐¹   48

        Equally similar to both. . . . ☐²

        More like Sansei . . . . ☐³

45. Would you say that generally the Nisei are not American enough, too American, or just about right? **(CHECK ONE)**

        Not American enough . . . . . ☐¹   49

        Just about right . . . . ☐²

        Too American . . . . ☐³

46. And what about the Sansei? Would you say that generally they are not American enough, too American, or just about right? **(CHECK ONE)**

        Not American enough . . . . . ☐¹   50

        Just about right . . . . ☐²

        Too American . . . . ☐³

47. Some people are talking about Sansei marrying Caucasians. How *important* a question do you think this is for the Sansei? Very important, rather important, rather unimportant, or very unimportant? **(CHECK ONE)**

        Very important . . . . ☐¹   51

        Rather important . . . . ☐²

        Rather unimportant . . . . . . ☐³

        Very unimportant . . . . ☐⁴

48. Speaking just for yourself now, do you think that on the whole the effect of Sansei marrying Caucasians is *good* for the Japanese Americans, *bad* for them, or do you think this will make *little difference* one way or the other? **(CHECK ONE)**

        Good for them . . . . ☐¹   52

        Make little difference . . . . ☐²

        Bad for them . . . . ☐³

49. In your opinion, should minority groups in America try to preserve something of the culture of their own group, or should they blend their culture into the mainstream of American life? **(CHECK ONE)**

        Preserve own culture . . . . . ☐¹   53

        Blend culture into
           mainstream . . . . ☐²

50. A. Do you suppose most Caucasians in America would be disturbed if a Japanese
American girl married a son of theirs? **(CHECK ONE)**

Caucasians would be disturbed . . . . □¹   54

Caucasians would not be disturbed . . . . . . □²

B. What if a Japanese American boy married a daughter of theirs? **(CHECK ONE)**

Caucasians would be disturbed . . . . □¹   55

Caucasians would not be disturbed . . . . . . □²

51. Now, we want to know a few things **(A** to **C)** about the people who are presently your
closest friends outside your immediate family – that is, the people whom you see most
often or feel closest to. Think for a moment of the *two* people you would say are your
closest friends. **PLEASE ENTER JUST THE *FIRST* NAME OF ONE OF THESE TWO
FRIENDS ON THE TOP OF THE FIRST COLUMN IN THE SPACE PROVIDED, AND
THE FIRST NAME OF THE OTHER ON TOP OF THE OTHER COLUMN. NOW ANSWER
FOR *EACH* FRIEND THE THREE QUESTIONS TO THE LEFT OF THE TWO COLUMNS.**

First name of first friend: First name of second friend:

	First friend	Second friend	
A. How did you get to know your friend? Did you become friends with him at school, at work, in some organization, in the neighborhood, in your family, through friends, or somewhere else. **(CHECK ONE FOR EACH FRIEND.)**	School........................ □¹ Work .... □² Organization .... □³ Neighborhood .... □⁴ Family .... □⁵ Friends .... □⁶ Another place .... □⁷ **(IF OTHER, WHAT?** _____)	School........................ □¹ Work .... □² Organization .... □³ Neighborhood .... □⁴ Family .... □⁵ Friends .... □⁶ Another place .... □⁷ **(IF OTHER, WHAT?** _____)	56 57
B. Is your friend a Nisei, a Sansei, a Yonsei, a Caucasian or of another background? **(CHECK ONE FOR EACH FRIEND)**	Nisei .... □¹ Sansei .... □² Yonsei .... □³ Caucasian .... □⁴ Other .... □⁵ **(IF OTHER, WHAT?** _____)	Nisei........................... □¹ Sansei .... □² Yonsei .... □³ Caucasian .... □⁴ Other .... □⁵ **(IF OTHER, WHAT?** _____)	58 59
C. What is your friend's occupation? Please tell a little about what he actually does on his job, and what industry he works in. **(ANSWER FOR EACH FRIEND IN APPROPRIATE BOX TO RIGHT)**			60-62 63-65

52. About how many groups or organizations do you belong to which have a more less regular membership and meet more or less regularly? In the count, please don't include any of the school organizations you have already told us about, or the church you may belong to: we'll come to that later. **(FILL IN NUMBER BELOW)**

_____ groups   66

53. **IF YOU BELONG TO ANY SUCH GROUPS, PLEASE ANSWER QUESTIONS 53 A, B, AND C; IF YOU BELONG TO NO GROUPS, SKIP TO QUESTION 54.**

   A. Of the groups you belong to, about how many have mostly Japanese American members? **(FILL IN NUMBER BELOW)**

_____ groups   67

   B. Are you now an officer or a committee member of any of the organizations you belong to? **(CHECK ONE)**

Yes .... ☐¹   68

No .... ☐²

   C. Of all the organizations you belong to, which is the one to which you devote the most time? **(PLEASE ENTER NAME OF THIS ORGANIZATION BELOW, AND DESCRIBE BRIEFLY WHAT IT DOES.)**

69-71

54. A. Which of the five things (**A** to **E**) listed below is *most* important for a Japanese American community leader today, as you see it? **(CHECK ONE IN LEFT-HAND COLUMN BELOW)**

   B. And which one do you think is the *least* important today? **(CHECK ONE IN THE RIGHT-HAND COLUMN BELOW)**

	A. Most important	**B.** Least important
A. Gaining concrete improvements for the Japanese American community	☐¹	☐¹
B. Joining with other groups to make a better America	☐²	☐²
C. Leading a virtuous life	☐³	☐³
D. Settling disputes and squabbles in the Japanese American community	☐⁴	☐⁴
E. Winning the respect of Caucasians	☐⁵	☐⁵

72
73

55. For questions A to DD on this and the next page, all we want to know is whether in general you agree or disagree with each of the statements. Please check an answer for each question, even if you are not sure of your answer. There are no right or wrong answers. All we want is the answer that comes to your mind first.

PLEASE DECIDE WHETHER *ON THE WHOLE* YOU AGREE OR DISAGREE WITH EACH STATEMENT. CHECK THE LEFT-HAND BOX IF YOU AGREE WITH THE STATEMENT, OR THE RIGHT-HAND BOX IF YOU DISAGREE.

DECK 04

	Agree	*Disagree*	
A. Most people in government are not really interested in problems of the average man	□¹	□²	11
B. I often get angry, irritated, or annoyed	□¹	□²	12
C. All a man should want out of life in the way of a career is a secure, not too difficult job, with enough pay to afford a nice car and eventually a home of his own	□¹	□²	13
D. The best way to judge a man is by his success in his profession	□¹	□²	14
E. The average man is probably better off today than he ever was	□¹	□²	15
F. I can usually just shrug my shoulders at misfortune	□¹	□²	16
G. If you try hard enough you usually get what you want	□¹	□²	17
H. Nowdays a person has to live pretty much for today and let tomorrow take care of itself	□¹	□²	18
I. When it comes to spending time, family demands come first	□¹	□²	19
J. When a man is born, the degree of success he is going to have is already in the cards, so he might just as well accept it and not fight against it	□¹	□²	20
K. Even today, the way you make money is more important than how much you make	□¹	□²	21
L. I often feel guilty about the things I do or don't do	□¹	□²	22
M. The art of work is finding an easier way	□¹	□²	23
N. Americans put too much stress on occupational success	□¹	□²	24
O. A man shouldn't try to change fate but to live with it	□¹	□²	25
P. I often worry about possible misfortunes	□¹	□²	26
Q. Most people can still be depended upon to come through in a pinch	□¹	□²	27
R. The secret of happiness is not expecting too much out of life and being content with what comes your way	□¹	□²	28
S. The family often asks too much of a person	□¹	□²	29
T. Next to health, money is the most important thing in life	□¹	□²	30
U. Although things may look hard at a particular moment, if you just bear up, things will usually improve	□¹	□²	31

V. Today success demands quantity, not quality . . . .   □¹   □²   32

W. The most important qualities of a real man are determination
    and driving ambition . . . .   □¹   □²   33

X. I sometimes can't help wondering if anything is worthwhile
    any more . . . .   □¹   □²   34

Y. I often feel frightened or afraid of things . . . .   □¹   □²   35

Z. The most important thing for a parent to do is to help his
    children get further ahead in the world than he did . . . .   □¹   □²   36

AA. Most people will go out of their way to help someone else . . . .   □¹   □²   37

BB. It's hardly fair to bring a child into the world today the
     way things look for the future . . . .   □¹   □²   38

CC. The best man is the one who puts his family above everything . . . . .   □¹   □²   39

DD. Anything I do I try to do well . . . .   □¹   □²   40

---

56. Below on the left is a list of statements (**A** to **F**) about jobs. In the first column, please decide
     which *one* of these you would want *most* in a job (WOMEN EVER MARRIED: in a job for your husband)
     and check the appropriate box. Choose which *one* you would want second most, and check the
     appropriate box. Go on ranking the remaining choices until you have recorded the *one* item you
     would want *least* in a job by checking one of the boxes in the right-hand column. **(CHECK A BOX
     REPRESENTING A *DIFFERENT STATEMENT* FOR EACH OF THE SIX RANKINGS.)**

	Most important	2nd most important	3rd most important	4th most important	5th most important	Least important	
A. Income is steady	□¹	□¹	□¹	□¹	□¹	□¹	41
B. Income is high	□²	□²	□²	□²	□²	□²	42
C. There is no danger of being fired or unemployed	□³	□³	□³	□³	□³	□³	43
D. Working hours are short, lots of free time	□⁴	□⁴	□⁴	□⁴	□⁴	□⁴	44
E. Chances of getting ahead are good	□⁵	□⁵	□⁵	□⁵	□⁵	□⁵	45
F. The work is important and gives a feeling of accomplishment	□⁶	□⁶	□⁶	□⁶	□⁶	□⁶	46

BREATHE DEEPLY. THANK YOU.

57. In your opinion, which is more often to blame if a person is poor – a lack of effort on his own part or circumstances beyond his control? **(CHECK ONE)**

Lack of own effort. . . . . . ☐¹ 47

Circumstances beyond
control . . . . ☐²

58. Who do you think has higher social value – people who make, buy, or sell things of practical use, or people like scholars and artists? **(CHECK ONE)**

Practical use . . . . ☐¹ 48

Scholars and artists . . . . . ☐²

59. If you think a thing is right, do you think you should go ahead and do it even if it is contrary to usual custom, or do you think it's better to follow custom? **(CHECK ONE)**

Go ahead . . . . ☐¹ 49

Follow custom . . . . ☐²

60. If you did not have any children, do you think you ought to adopt a child to continue the family line even if the child were not related to you, or do you think you need not do that? **(CHECK ONE)**

Should adopt . . . . ☐¹ 50

Need not adopt . . . . ☐²

We want to find out a little about what you think about the history and position of the Japanese in America.

61. Below is a list of some ways (A to D) in which discrimination against Japanese Americans is said to have occurred. Will you please try to remember whether in the past ten years or so you or your immediate family have experienced any of these forms of discrimination *personally?* Next, for any of these forms of discrimination you haven't experienced personally, would you please try to remember if you have *heard about* cases in which other Japanese Americans experienced it within the past ten years? **(CHECK THE BOX IN THE APPROPRIATE COLUMN FOR EACH OF THE FORMS OF DISCRIMINATION)**

	Experienced *personally*	*Not* experienced, but *heard* about	*Neither* experienced *nor* heard about	
A. Discrimination in housing	☐¹	☐²	☐³	51
B. Discrimination in schools	☐¹	☐²	☐³	52
C. Discrimination in jobs	☐¹	☐²	☐³	53
D. Police brutality	☐¹	☐²	☐³	54

62. How much do you think that being a Japanese American has hindered your advancement —
    not at all, only a little, somewhat, or very much? **(CHECK ONE)**

    Not at all . . . . ☐ 1   55

    Only a little . . . . ☐ 2

    Somewhat . . . . ☐ 3

    Very much . . . . ☐ 4

63. How much do you think that being Japanese American has hindered *your parents'* advance-
    ment — not at all, only a little, somewhat, or very much? **(CHECK ONE)**

    Not at all . . . . ☐ 1   56

    Only a little . . . . ☐ 2

    Somewhat . . . . ☐ 3

    Very much . . . . ☐ 4

64. Observers have offered many different explanations for hostility shown to the Issei in the
    period after they arrived in this country. How do *you* account for this hostility? **(ANSWER
    BELOW)**

                                                                                              57

                                                                                              58

                                                                                              59

65. After the United States entered World War II, Japanese Americans from the West Coast
    were placed in relocation camps. As you think back about what you know of this action,
    why would you say it was done? **(ANSWER BELOW)**

                                                                                              60

                                                                                              61

                                                                                              62

66. During the World War II relocation, some Nisei worked to make relocation as orderly and comfortable as possible, while others protested the injustice of the relocation and tried to have it declared unconstitutional. Which kind of leader do you *now* think employed the better approach? **(CHECK ONE)**

Orderly and comfortable . . . ☐¹

Protest . . . . ☐²

63

67. Members of many minority groups in America have complained that their groups are not being treated as full and equal Americans. Which of the groups listed below **(A to G)** can rightfully complain that they are not being treated as full and equal Americans today? **(CHECK ONE FOR EACH GROUP)**

DECK 05

	Can rightfully complain	Cannot rightfully complain	
A. Negroes	☐¹	☐²	11
B. Italian Americans	☐¹	☐²	12
C. Japanese Americans	☐¹	☐²	13
D. Chinese Americans	☐¹	☐²	14
E. Jews	☐¹	☐²	15
F. Mexican Americans	☐¹	☐²	16
G. Puerto Ricans	☐¹	☐²	1⁷

68. Assume that you are a houseowner and a qualified Negro wished to buy your house:

A. If your neighbors didn't disapprove would you sell your house to a Negro? **(CHECK ONE)**

Yes . . . . ☐¹

No . . . . ☐²

18

B. If your neighbors disapproved of your selling your house to such a Negro, would you sell it to him? **(CHECK ONE)**

Yes . . . . ☐¹

No . . . . ☐²

19

C. Would *you* disapprove if a neighbor wished to sell *his* house to a qualified Negro?

Yes . . . . ☐¹

No . . . . ☐²

20

69. Now assume that it was a qualified Mexican American who wished to buy your house:

   A. If your neighbors didn't disapprove would you sell your house to a Mexican American? **(CHECK ONE)**

   Yes . . . . ☐¹   *21*

   No. . . . . ☐²

   B. If your neighbors disapproved of your selling your house to such a Mexican American, would you sell it to him? **(CHECK ONE)**

   Yes . . . . ☐¹   *22*

   No . . . . ☐²

   C. Would *you* disapprove if a neighbor wished to sell *his* house to a qualified Mexican American?

   Yes . . . . ☐¹   *23*

   No . . . . ☐²

70. A. Negroes are interested in bettering their position in American society. What advice would you give Negroes, as a race, to achieve their goals? **(ANSWER BELOW)**

                                                                                              24

                                                                                              25

                                                                                              26

   B. How long do you think it will take for the Negroes to achieve their goals? **(FILL IN BELOW)**

                                                   _____ years   *27*

   C. What will keep them from achieving their goals sooner than this? **(ANSWER BELOW)**

                                                                                              28

                                                                                              29

                                                                                              30

71. People nowadays are talking about "black power." Would you say that on the whole you are very favorable to the idea of "black power," somewhat favorable, somewhat unfavorable, or very unfavorable; or would you say you have no opinion one way or the other? **(CHECK ONE)**

   Very favorable . . . . ☐¹   *31*

   Somewhat favorable . . . . . ☐²

   Somewhat unfavorable . . . . ☐³

   Very unfavorable . . . . ☐⁴

   No opinion . . . . ☐⁵

72. Now, we want to find out something about your religious affiliations. Are you a Buddhist, a Protestant, a Roman Catholic, or something else; or do you not identify yourself with any religion?

Buddhist . . . . ☐¹   32

Protestant . . . . ☐²

Roman Catholic . . . . ☐³

Other (what?) . . . . ☐⁴

No religious
identification . . . . ☐⁵

73. Have you at an earlier time been a member of a different religion? **(CHECK ONE)**

Yes . . . . ☐¹   33

No **(GO TO QUESTION 74)** . . . . ☐²

IF YES, ANSWER: A. What religion was the *first* one you belonged to? **(CHECK ONE)**

Buddhist . . . . ☐¹   34

Protestant . . . . ☐²

Roman Catholic . . . . ☐³

Other (what?) _____

_____ ☐⁴

IF YOU ARE NOW A BUDDHIST, ANSWER QUESTION 74A. IF YOU ARE NOW A PROTESTANT, ANSWER QUESTION 74B. IF YOU ARE NEITHER A BUDDHIST NOR A PROTESTANT, SKIP TO QUESTION 75.

74A. Which Buddhist sect are you a member of? **(FILL IN BELOW)**

_____
(sect)   35-36

74B. Which Protestant denomination are you a member of? **(FILL IN BELOW)**

_____
(denomination)

75. How often do you usually attend religious services – once a week, a few times a month, once a month, or less often? **(CHECK ONE)**

Once a week or more . . . . . ☐¹

Few times a month . . . . . . ☐²

Once a month . . . . ☐³

Less often than that . . . . . ☐⁴

76. Aside from attendance at religious services, how important would you say religion is to you – very important, fairly important, or not important at all? **(CHECK ONE)**

Very important . . . . ☐¹

Fairly important . . . . ☐²

Not important at all . . . . . . ☐³

IF YOU HAVE EVER BEEN MARRIED, ANSWER QUESTION 77. OTHERWISE SKIP TO QUESTION 78.

77. What religion does your spouse belong to? Is he (she) a Buddhist, a Protestant, a Roman Catholic, or something else; or does she have no religious identification? **(CHECK ONE)**

Buddhist . . . . ☐¹

Protestant . . . . ☐²

Roman Catholic . . . . ☐³

Other (what?) . . . . ☐⁴

No religious
identification . . . . ☐⁵

EVERYONE ANSWER:

78. Which political party do you generally favor in national elections? **(CHECK ONE)**

Democratic . . . . ☐¹

Republican . . . . ☐²

Independent . . . . ☐³

Other (what?) _____
_____ ☐⁴

79. Generally speaking, how much interest would you say you have in politics – a great deal, a fair amount, only a little, or no interest at all? **(CHECK ONE)**

A great deal . . . . ☐¹

A fair amount . . . . ☐²

Only a little . . . . ☐³

No interest at all . . . . ☐⁴

80. During the last few months, has anyone outside your family asked you for advice about politics or public affairs? **(CHECK ONE)**

Yes . . . . □¹   42

No . . . . □²

81. What magazines do you subscribe to or regularly read? **(FILL OUT LIST BELOW)**

1. _____   6. _____   43

2. _____   7. _____

3. _____   8. _____   44

4. _____   9. _____

5. _____   10. _____   45

82. How often do you read Japanese American newspapers? Do you read them regularly, occasionally, hardly ever, or do you never read a Japanese American newspaper? **(CHECK ONE)**

Regularly . . . . □¹   46

Occasionally . . . . □²

Hardly ever . . . . □³

Never . . . . □⁴

83. Are you able to speak Japanese quite fluently, pretty well, only a little, or not at all? **(CHECK ONE)**

Quite fluently **(GO TO QUESTION 84)** . . . . □¹   47

Pretty well **(ANSWER A)** . . . . □²

Only a little **(ANSWER A)** . . . . □³

Not at all **(ANSWER A)** . . . . □⁴

A. Do you wish you could speak Japanese better than you do? **(CHECK ONE)**

Yes . . . . □¹   48

No . . . . □²

84. Have you ever been to Japan?

Yes . . . . □¹   49

No . . . . □²

85. While you were growing up, how much training or instruction in Japanese culture would you say you had: a great deal, some, only a little, or none at all?

A great deal . . . . ·1   30

Some . . . . ·2

Only a little . . . . ·3

None at all . . . . ·4

▶ **PLEASE ANSWER:** A. Did you receive this training or instruction at home, outside the home, or both in and outside the home?

At home . . . . ·1   31

Outside the home . . . . ·2

Both in and outside
the home . . . . ·3

86. Do you think you know enough about Japanese culture, or do you believe that you ought to know more than you do?

Know enough . . . . ·1   32

Ought to know more . . . . . ·2

87. Has you or your spouse ever been a member of a labor union ? **(CHECK ONE)**

Yes . . . . ·1   33

No . . . . ·2

88. Has you or your spouse ever served in the United States armed forces, active or reserve?
(CHECK ONE)

Yes . . . . ·1   34

No . . . . ·2

89. We are interested in knowing whether, before filling out this questionnaire, you had heard anything about the *actual content* of some of the questions on it. **(CHECK ONE)**

Heard about content of some of
the questions . . . . ·1   35

Had not heard about content . . . . ·2

A peek at the facing page will reveal that YOU ARE FINISHED. We cannot sufficiently thank you for your con-   56
tribution to our study. We apologize for putting you through so much, but hope you have had some fun, too. As
you know, we are EAGER to receive your finished questionnaire.   57

PLEASE BE SURE YOU PLACE THE QUESTIONNAIRE RIGHT AWAY INTO THE POSTAGE-PAID RETURN   58
ENVELOPE, AND MAIL IT AS SOON AS POSSIBLE. YOUR FILLED-OUT QUESTIONNAIRE IS INVALUABLE
TO US.

Please use the COMMENTS page to enlighten us further, to protest individual questions, or to curse us, as you wish. THANK YOU AGAIN.

Bibliography

Bibliography

Adams, Bert N.
 1968   *Kinship in an Urban Setting.* Chicago: Markham.
Adams, Romanzo C.
 1937   *Interracial Marriage in Hawaii.* New York: MacMillan.
Bales, Robert F.
 1970   *Personality and Interpersonal Behavior.* New York: Holt, Rine-
         hart, and Winston.
Bales, Robert F., A. Paul Hare, and Edgar F. Borgatta (eds.)
 1965   *Small Groups: Studies in Social Interaction.* Revised Edition.
         New York: Knopf.
Barber, Bernard
 1957   *Social Stratification.* New York: Harcourt, Brace.
Barker, George C.
 1947   "Social functions of language in a Mexican-American com-
         munity." *Acta Americana* 5 (February):185-202.
Barron, M.
 1972   *The Blending Americans, Patterns of Intermarriage.* Chicago:
         Quadrangle.
 1975   "Recent developments in minority and race relations."
         Annals 420 (July):125-176.
Barth, Frederick.
 1969   *Ethnic Groups and Boundaries.* Boston: Little, Brown.
Benedict, Ruth
 1946   *The Chrysanthemum and the Sword.* New York: Houghton.
Benson, L.E.
 1946   "Mail surveys can be valuable." *Public Opinion Quarterly* 10
         (Summer):234-241.

Bernard, Jessie
   1973   *The Sociology of Community.* Glenview, Ill.: Scott, Foresman.
Bloom, Leonard, and Ruth Reimer
   1949   *Removal and Return: The Socio-Economic Effects of the War on Japanese Americans.* Berkeley: University of California Press.
Bonacich, Edna M.
   1972   "A theory of ethnic antagonism: the split labor market." *American Sociological Review* 37 (October):547-559.
   1973   "A theory of middleman minorities." *American Sociological Review* 38 (October):583-594.
   1975   "Small business and Japanese American ethnic solidarity." *Amerasia Journal* 3 (Summer):96-112.
Brody, Eugene B.
   1968   *Minority Group Adolescents in the United States.* Baltimore: Williams & Wilkins.
Brooks, M. S., and K. Kunihiro
   1952   "Education in the assimilation of Japanese: a study in the Houston area of Texas." *Sociology and Social Research* 27 (September-October):16-22.
Bruce, J.M.
   1970   "Intragenerational occupational mobility and visiting with kin and friend." *Social Forces* 49 (September):117-127.
Bush, Lewis
   1968   *77 Samurai: Japan's First Embassy to America.* Tokyo and Palo Alto, California: Kodansha International.
Cannell, Charles F., and Floyd J. Fowler
   1963   "Comparison of a self-enumerative procedure and a personal interview: a validity study." *Public Opinion Quarterly* 27 (2) (Summer):250-264.
Caudill, William
   1952   "Japanese-American personality and acculturation." *Genetic Psychology Monographs* 45, Part 1 (February):3-101.
Caudill, William, and George DeVos
   1956   "Achievement, culture and personality: the case of the Japanese Americans." *American Anthropologist* 58:1102-1126.
Child, Irvin L.
   1943   *Italian or American: The Second Generation in Conflict.* New Haven: Yale University Press.
Chuman, Frank F.
   1976   *The Bamboo People: The Law and Japanese Americans.* Del Mar, California: Publishers, Inc.

Cohen, Steven Martin
1977 "Socioeconomic determinants of intraethnic marriage and friendship." *Social Forces* 55 (June):997-1010.
Colombotos, J.
1965 "The effects of personal vs. telephone interviews on socially acceptable responses." Paper presented at the annual meeting of the American Association for Public Opinion Research, Groton.
1969 "Personal vs. telephone interviews: effect on responses." *Public Health Report* 84 (September):773-782.
Connor, John W.
1974a "Acculturation and family continuities in three generations of Japanese Americans." *Journal of Marriage and the Family* 36 (1) (February):159-165.
1974b "Value continuities and change in three generations of Japanese Americans." *Ethos* 2 (Fall):232-264.
1977 *Tradition and Change in Three Generations of Japanese Americans.* Chicago: Nelson-Hall.
Conrat, Masie, and Richard Conrat
1972 *Executive Order 9066: The Internment of 110,000 Japanese Americans.* Los Angeles: California Historical Society.
Conroy, Hilary, and T. Scott Miyakawa (eds.)
1973 *East Across the Pacific.* Santa Barbara California: CLIO Press.
Daniels, Roger
1968 *The Politics of Prejudice.* New York: Athenum.
Davis, James A.
1971 *Elementary Survey Analysis.* Englewood Cliffs, N.J.: Prentice-Hall.
DeFleur, Melvin L., and Chang-Soo Cho
1957 "Assimilation of Japanese-born women in an American city." *Social Problems* 4 (3) (January):244-257.
DeVos, George A.
1973 *Socialization for Achievement: Essays on the Cultural Psychology of the Japanese.* Berkeley and Los Angeles: University of California Press.
Dohrenwend, Bruce P., and Robert J. Smith
1962 "Toward a theory of acculturation." *Southwestern Journal of Anthropology* 18 (Spring):30-39.
Dore, R. P.
1971 *City Life in Japan: A Study of a Tokyo Ward.* Berkeley and Los Angeles: University of California Press.

Embree, J.F.
   1941   "Acculturation among the Japanese of Kona, Hawaii."
           Memoirs of the American Anthropological Association, Vol.
           59.
Fairchild, Henry Pratt
   1911   *Greek Immigration to the United States.* New Haven: Yale
           University Press.
Feagin, Joe R., and Nancy Fujitaki
   1972   "On the assimilation of Japanese Americans." *Amerasia Jour-
           nal* 1:13-30.
Fellows, Donald K.
   1972   *A Mosaic of America's Ethnic Minorities.* New York: John
           Wiley and Sons.
Fong, Stanley L. M.
   1965   "Assimilation of Chinese in America: changes in orienta-
           tion and social perception." *American Journal of Sociology* 71
           (November):265-275.
Glazer, Nathan, and Daniel P. Moynihan
   1970   *Beyond the Melting Pot.* Cambridge: M.I.T. Press.
Goldstein, Sidney, and Calvin Goldscheider
   1968   *Jewish Americans: Three Generations in a Jewish Community.*
           Englewood Cliffs, N.J.: Prentice-Hall.
Gordon, Albert I.
   1949   *Jews in Transition.* Minneapolis: University of Minnesota
           Press.
Gordon, Milton
   1964   *Assimilation in American Life.* New York: Oxford University
           Press.
   1975   "Toward a general theory of racial and ethnic group
           relations." Pp. 84-110 in N. Glazer and D. P. Moyni-
           han (eds.), *Ethnicity.* Cambridge: Harvard University
           Press.
Hagopian, Elaine C., and Ann Paden (eds.)
   1969   *The Arab-Americans: Studies in Assimilation.* Wilmette, Illi-
           nois: Medina University Press International.
Handlin, Oscar
   1961   "Historical perspectives on the American ethnic group."
           Daedalus (Spring):220-232.
Hansell, Stephen, and Fred L. Strodtbeck
   1973   "Ego development scores obtained during home visits and
           in concomitant phone interviews." Unpublished manu-
           script, University of Chicago.

Hansen, M.
  1952   "The third generation in America." *Commentary* 14 (5) (November):492-503.
Herberg, Will
  1955   *Protestant, Catholic, Jew.* New York: Doubleday.
Herskovits, Melville J.
  1958   *Acculturation: The Study of Culture Contact.* Goucester, Maine: Peter Smith.
Hillery, George A., Jr.
  1955   "Definitions of community: areas of agreement." *Rural Sociology* 20:194-204.
Hirschman, Charles
  1975   *Ethnic and Social Stratification in Peninsular Malaysia.* Arnold M. and Caroline Rose Monograph. Washington, D.C.: American Sociological Association.
Hokubei Mainichi Yearbook
  1964   San Francisco: Hokubei Mainichi Shinbunsha.
Homans, George C.
  1961   *Social Behavior: Its Elementary Forms.* New York: Harcourt, Brace, and World.
Horinouchi, Isao
  1967   "Educational values and preadaption in the acculturation of the Japanese Americans." *Sacramento Anthropological Society,* Paper 7 (Fall):1-60.
Hosokawa, William K.
  1969   *Nisei: The Quiet Americans.* New York: William Morrow.
Humphrey, Norman D.
  1944   "The Detroit Mexican immigrant and naturalization." *Social Forces* 22 (March):332-335.
Hundley, Norris, Jr.
  1976   *The Asian American: The Historical Experience.* Santa Barbara, California: CLIO Press.
Ianni, Francis A.J.
  1952   The Acculturation of the Italo-Americans in Norristown, Pennsylvania. Unpublished dissertation, Pennsylvania State University.
  1957   "Residential and occupational mobility as indices of the acculturation of an ethnic group." *Social Forces* 36 (October): 65-72.
Ichihashi, Y.
  1932   *Japanese in the United States.* Stanford, California: Stanford University Press.

Iga, Mamoru
    1957   "The Japanese social structure and the source of mental
            strains of Japanese immigrants in the United States." *Social
            Forces* 35 (March):271-278.
Johnston, R.
    1969   *The Assimilation Myth.* The Hague: Martinus Nijhoff.
Kagiwada, George
    1968   "The third generation hypothesis: structural assimilation
            among Japanese-Americans." Paper presented at the an-
            nual meeting of the Pacific Sociological Association, San
            Francisco, March.
Kiefer, Christie
    1974   *Changing Cultures, Changing Lives.* San Francisco: Jossey-Bass.
Kikumura, Akemi, and Harry H. L. Kitano
    1973   "Interracial marriage: a picture of the Japanese-
            Americans." *Journal of Social Issues* 29 (2):67-81.
Kitano, Harry H. L.
    1969   *Japanese Americans: The Evolution of a Subculture.* Englewood
            Cliffs, N.J.: Prentice-Hall.
    1972   "Japanese-Americans on the road to dissent." Pp. 93-113 in
            Joe Boskin and R. Rosenstone (eds.), *Seasons of Rebellion.*
            New York: Holt, Rinehart & Winston.
    1974   *Race Relations.* Englewood Cliffs, N.J.: Prentice-Hall.
    1976   *Japanese Americans: The Evolution of a Subculture.* 2nd Edition.
            Englewood Cliffs, N.J.: Prentice-Hall.
Klatzky, Sheila R.
    1972   *Patterns of Contact with Relatives.* Arnold M. and Caroline
            Rose Monograph. Washington, D.C.: American Socio-
            logical Association.
Kramer, Judith R.
    1970   *The American Minority Community.* New York: Thomas
            Y. Crowell.
Kurokawa, Minako
    1970   *Minority Responses.* New York: Random House.
Kwan, Kian M.
    1958   Assimilation of the Chinese in the United States: An Ex-
            ploratory Study in California. Unpublished Ph.D. disserta-
            tion, University of California, Berkeley.
Lebra, Takie Sugiyama
    1972   "Acculturation dilemma: the function of Japanese moral
            values for Americanization." *Council on Anthropology and Educa-
            tion Newsletter* 3:6-13.

1976   *Japanese Patterns of Behavior.* Honolulu: University of Hawaii Press.

Lenski, Gerhard
1963   *The Religious Factor.* Garden City, N.Y.: Anchor Books.

Levine, Gene N., and Edna M. Bonacich
1970   "Non-individual units in the analysis of surveys: the case of the Japanese American Research Project." Paper presented at the annual meeting of the Pacific Chapter of the American Association for Public Opinion Research.

Levine, Gene N., and Darrel Montero
1973   "Socioeconomic mobility among three generations of Japanese Americans." *Journal of Social Issues* 29 (2):33-48.

1975   "Review of William Petersen's Japanese Americans." *Contemporary Sociology* 4 (July):417-419.

Lieberson, Stanley
1961   "The impact of residential segregation on ethnic assimilation." *Social Forces* 40 (1) (October):52-57.

Light, Ivan H.
1972   *Ethnic Enterprise in America: Business and Welfare among Chinese, Japanese, and Blacks.* Berkeley and Los Angeles: University of California Press.

Lind, Andrew W.
1967   *Hawaii's People.* 3rd Edition. Honolulu: University of Hawaii Press.

Linton, Ralph
1963   *Acculturation in Seven Indian Tribes.* Goucester, Maine: Peter Smith.

Lipset, Seymour M.
1950   "Changing social status and prejudice: the race relations theories of a pioneering American sociologist." *Commentary* 9 (May):475-479.

Lipset, Seymour M., and Reinhard Bendix
1959   *Social Mobility in Industrial Society.* Berkeley: University of California Press.

Lopata, Helena Znaniecki
1976   *Polish Americans.* Englewood Cliffs, N.J.: Prentice-Hall.

Lopreato, Joseph
1970   *Italian Americans.* New York: Random House.

Lyman, Stanford M.
1968   "The race relations cycle of Robert E. Park." *Pacific Sociological Review* 2 (Spring):16-22.

1970a   *The Asian in the West.* Social Science and Humanities Publica-
         tion No. 4. Reno: University of Nevada Press.
1970b   "Contrasts in the community organization of Chinese and
         Japanese in North America." Pp. 57-63 in Stanford M.
         Lyman (ed.),   *The Asian in the West.* Social Science and
         Humanities Publication No. 4. Reno: University of Nevada
         Press.
1973   *The Black American in Sociological Thought.* New York: Capricorn
         Books.
1974   *Chinese Americans.* New York: Random House.
1977   *The Asian in North America.* Santa Barbara, California: CLIO
         Press.

Masuda, Minoru, Gary H. Matsumoto, and Gerald M. Meredith
1970   "Ethnic identity in three generations of Japanese Amer-
         icans." *Journal of Social Psychology* 81 (2nd half) (August):
         199-207.

Meredith, Gerald M.
1966   "Amae and acculturation among Japanese college students in
         Hawaii." *Journal of Social Psychology* 70:171-180.

Meredith, Gerald M., and C.G.W. Meredith
1966   "Acculturation and personality among Japanese-American
         college students in Hawaii." *Journal of Social Psychology*
         68:175-182.

Merton, Robert K.
1941   "Intermarriage and social structure: fact and theory." *Psy-
         chiatry* 4 (August):361-374.
1957   *Social Theory and Social Structure.* Glencoe, Illinois: Free
         Press.

Miyakawa, T. Scott, and Yasuo Sakata
1974   "Japan in dislocation and emigration: the demographic
         background of American immigration." In Donald Fleming
         and B. Bailyn (eds.), *Perspectives in American History,* Volume
         VII. Cambridge: Harvard University Press.

Miyamoto, S. Frank
1939   "Social solidarity among the Japanese in Seattle." *University of
         Washington Publications in the Social Sciences,* 11(2)
         (December):57-130.

Miyamoto, S. Frank, and Robert O'Brien
1947   "A survey of some changes in the Seattle Japanese community
         since evacuation." *Research Studies of the State College of
         Washington* 15 (June):147-154.

Modell, John
    1977   *The Economics and Politics of Racial Accommodation: The Japanese of Los Angeles, 1900-1942.* Urbana, Illinois: University of Illinois Press.

Montero, Darrel
    1974a   "Correlates of achievement orientation among a national sample of second generation Japanese Americans." Paper presented at the annual meeting of the Pacific Sociological Association, San Jose, California.

    1974b   "A study of social desirability response bias: The mail questionnaire, the face-to-face interview, and the telephone interview compared." Paper presented at the annual meeting of the American Sociological Association, Montreal.

    1976a   "Response effects in a national survey." Paper presented at the annual meeting of the American Sociological Association, New York.

    1976b   "Issues on conducting research in minority communities." Paper presented at the annual meeting of the American Sociological Association, New York.

    1977   Intermarriage among Three Generations of Japanese Americans. Unpublished manuscript, University of Maryland, College Park.

    1978   "For Japanese Americans, Erosion." *The New York Times,* (December 4): A21.

    1979   *Vietnamese Americans: Patterns of Resettlement and Socioeconomic Adaptation in the United States.* Boulder, Colorado: Westview Press.

    1979   "Vietnamese Refugees in America: Toward a Theory of Spontaneous International Migration." *International Migration Review* 13 (4)

    1980   "The Elderly Japanese American: Aging among the First Generation Immigrants." *Genetic Psychology Monographs,* in press.

Montero, Darrel, and Gene N. Levine
    1974   "Third generation Japanese Americans." Paper presented at the annual meeting of the Pacific Sociological Association, San Jose, California.

    1977   (eds.). "Research among Racial and Cultural Minorities: Problems, Prospects, and Pitfalls." *Journal of Social Issues* 33 (4): entire issue.

Montero, Darrel, and Judith McDowell
   1979   "Refugees: Making It." *The New York Times,* (March 12):A17.
Montero, Darrel, and Ronald Tadao Tsukashima
   1977   "Assimilation and educational achievement: the case of the second generation Japanese American." *Sociological Quarterly* 18 (Autumn):490-503.
Moore, Joan W.
   1976   *Mexican Americans.* 2nd Edition. Englewood Cliffs, N.J.: Prentice-Hall.
Murdock, G. P.
   1957   "World ethnographic sample." *American Anthropologist* 59: 664-687.
Obidinski, Eugene
   1968   Ethnic to Status Group: A Study of Polish Americans in Buffalo. Unpublished dissertation, State University of New York.
Office of Population Research
   1965   "Japanese immigrants in Brazil." *Population Index* 31 (2) (April):117-38.
Ogawa, Dennis
   1971   *From Japs to Japanese: An Evolution of Japanese-American Stereotypes.* Berkeley: McCutchan.
Park, Robert E.
   1914   "Racial assimilation in secondary groups." *Publications of the American Sociological Society* 8:66-72.
   1950   *Race and Culture.* Glencoe, Illinois: The Free Press.
Park, Robert E., and Ernest W. Burgess
   1924   *Introduction to the Science of Sociology.* Chicago: University of Chicago Press.
Park, Robert E., and Herbert A. Miller
   1921   *Old World Traits Transplanted.* New York: Harper & Brothers.
Petersen, William
   1970   "Success story: Japanese American style." Pp. 169-178 in Minako Kurokawa (ed.), *Minority Responses.* New York: Random House.
   1971   *Japanese Americans: Oppression and Success.* New York: Random House.
Rinder, Irwin D.
   1953   Jewish Identification and the Race Relations Cycle. Unpublished Ph.D. dissertation, University of Chicago.

Roos, Patricia A.
  1977   "Questioning the stereotypes: explaining differentials in in-
          come attainment of Japanese, Mexican Americans, and Ang-
          los in California." Presented at the annual meeting of the
          American Sociological Association, New York.
Rosen, Bernard C.
  1959   "Race, ethnicity, and the achievement syndrome." *American
          Sociological Review* 24:47-60.
Roy, Prodipto
  1962   "The measurement of assimilation: the Spokane Indians."
          American Journal of Sociology 67 (March):541-551.
Sakata, Y.
  Forth- Japanese Immigration to the United States. Dissertation in
  coming progress, University of California, Los Angeles.
Sandberg, Neil C.
  1974   *Ethnic Identity and Assimilation: The Polish American Community.*
          New York: Praeger.
Schmid, Calvin E., and Charles E. Nobbe
  1965   "Socioeconomic differentials among non-white races." *American
          Sociological Review* 30 (December):909-922.
Schneider, David M., and George C. Homans
  1955   "Kinship terminology and the American kinship system."
          American Anthropologist 57:1194-1208.
Schwartz, A. J.
  1970   *Traditional Values and Contemporary Achievement of Japanese-
          American Pupils.* Center for the Study of Evaluation, Report
          No. 65. Los Angeles: University of California.
  1971   "The culturally advantaged: a study of Japanese-American
          pupils." *Sociology and Social Research* 55 (3) (April):341-353.
Senter, Donovan, and Florence Hawley
  1946   "The grammar school as the basic acculturating influence for
          native New Mexicans." *Social Forces* 24 (May):398-
          407.
Simirenko, Alex
  1964   *Pilgrims, Colonists, and Frontiersmen: An Ethnic Community in
          Transition.* Glencoe, Illinois: The Free Press.
Smith, Bradford
  1948   *Americans from Japan.* Philadelphia: Lippincott.
Spiro, Melford E.
  1955   "The acculturation of American ethnic groups." *American An-
          thropologist* 57 (December):1240-1252.

Steiner, Jesse F.
  1917   *The Japanese Invasion.* Chicago: A. C. McClurg.
Strodtbeck, Fred L.
  1958   "Family interaction, values, and achievement." Pp. 147-165 in
            Marshall Sklare (ed.), *The Jews: Social Patterns of an American
            Group.* Glencoe, Illinois: The Free Press.
Strong, Edward K., Jr.
  1934   *The Second Generation Japanese Problem.* Palo Alto, California:
            Stanford University Press.
Stuckert, Robert P.
  1963   "Occupational mobility and family relationships." *Social Forces*
            41 (March):301-307.
Sudman, Seymour, and Norman M. Bradburn
  1974   *Response Effects in Surveys.* Chicago: Aldine.
Sue, Stanley, and Harry H. L. Kitano, eds.
  1973   "Asian Americans: A Success Story?" *Journal of Social Issues* 29
            (2): entire volume.
Taft, Ronald
  1957   "A psychological model for the study of social assimilation."
            Human Relations 10:141-156.
Takagi, Paul T.
  1967   "The influence of parental origin upon Nisei educational
            attainment." Revised version of paper presented to the
            Kroeber Anthropological Society, Tenth Annual Meeting,
            1966.
Tax, Sol (ed.)
  1967   *Acculturation in the Americas.* New York: Cooper Square
            Publishers.
Thomas, Dorothy S., and Richard Nishimoto
  1969   *The Spoilage.* Berkeley and Los Angeles: University of Cali-
            fornia Press. (Originally published in 1946.)
Tinker, John N.
  1972   "Intermarriage and ethnic boundaries: the Japanese-Ameri-
            can case." Paper presented at the annual meeting of the Pacific
            Sociological Association, Portland.
  1973   "Intermarriage and ethnic boundaries: the Japanese Amer-
            ican case." *Journal of Social Issues* 29 (2):49-66.
Tönnies, Ferdinand
  1957   *Community and Society.* East Lansing: Michigan State Uni-
            versity Press (Originally published in German in 1887 under
            the title, *Gemeinschaft und Gesellschaft*). Translated by Charles P.
            Loomis.

Toth, Robert C.
  1977   "Japanese in U.S. outdo Horatio Alger." *Los Angeles Times* (October 17):1,10-11.
Tsukashima, Ronald Tadao, and Darrel Montero
  1976   "The contact hypothesis: social and economic contact and generational changes in the study of Black anti-Semitism." *Social Forces* 55 (September):149-165.
Ueda, Reed
  1974   "The Americanization and education of Japanese-Americans." Pp. 71-90 in Edgar G. Epps (ed.), *Cultural Pluralism.* Berkeley, California: McCutchan.
U.S. Bureau of the Census
  1963a   *Non-White Population by Race.* Final report PC(2)-1C. Washington, D.C.: U.S. Government Printing Office.
  1963b   *Detailed Characteristics. U.S. Summary.* Final report PC(1)-1D. Washington, D.C.: U.S. Government Printing Office.
  1963c   *Census of Population: 1960, Occupational Characteristics.* Subject Report (1963: Table 1) Washington, D.C.: U.S. Government Printing Office.
  1970a   *Census of Population: 1970, General Population Characteristics.* U.S. Summary. PCV(2)-1. Washington, D.C.: U.S. Government Printing Office.
  1970b   *Marital Status.* Subject Report PC-2-4C. Washington, D.C.: U.S. Government Printing Office.
  1971   *General Population Characteristics.* Final report PC(1)-B13 Hawaii. Washington, D.C.: U.S. Government Printing Office.
  1972   *Census of Population: 1970, Occupation by Industry.* (1972: Table 1) Washington, D.C.: U.S. Government Printing Office.
  1973a   *Characteristics of the Population. U.S. Summary.* v.1, pt. 1, sec. 2. Washington, D.C.: U.S. Government Printing Office.
  1973b   *American Indians.* Subject Report PC(2)-1F. Washington, D.C.: U.S. Government Printing Office.
  1973c   *Negro Population.* Subject Report PC(2)-1B. Washington, D.C.: U.S. Government Printing Office.
  1973d   *Japanese, Chinese and Filipinos in the United States.* Subject Report PC(2)-1G. Washington, D.C.: U.S. Government Printing Office.
U.S. Department of Health, Education, and Welfare
  1974   *A Study of Selected Socio-Economic Characteristics of Ethnic*

Minorities Based on the 1970 Census, Volume II: Asian Americans.
HEW (OS) 75-121 (July). Washington, D.C.: U.S. Government Printing Office.

Uyeki, Eugene S.
1960   "Correlates of ethnic identification." *American Journal of Sociology* 65 (5) March:468-474.

Van den Berghe, Pierre
1972   *Intergroup Relations: Sociological Perspectives.* New York: Basic Books.

Varon, Barbara F.
1967   "The Japanese Americans: comparative occupational status, 1960 and 1950." *Demography* 4:809-819.

Vlachos, Evangelos C.
1969   *Assimilation of Greeks in the United States.* Greece: National Centre of Social Researches Publications.

Warner, W. Lloyd
1949   *Democracy in Jonesville.* New York: Harper and Bros.

Warner, W. Lloyd, and Leo Srole
1945   *The Social Systems of American Ethnic Groups.* New Haven: Yale University Press.

Watson, James B., and Julian Samora
1944   "Subordinate leadership in a bicultural community: an analysis." *American Sociological Review* 19 (August):413-421.

Weiss, Melford S.
1974   *Valley City: A Chinese Community in America.* Cambridge, Mass.: Schenkman.

Whyte, William Foote
1943   *Street Corner Society.* Chicago: University of Chicago Press.

Williams, Robin M., Jr.
1975   "Race and ethnic relations." Pp. 125-164 in Alex Inkeles, James Coleman, and Neil Smelser (eds.), *Annual Review of Sociology,* Volume 1. Palo Alto, California: Annual Reviews, Inc.

Wilson, Robert A.
Forth-   *The History of the Japanese in the United States.* University of
coming   California, Los Angeles.

Wittke, Carl
1956   *The Irish in America.* Baton Rouge: Louisiana State University Press.

Yamamoto, Joe
1968   "Japanese American identity crisis." Pp. 133-156 in Eugene

B. Brody (ed.), *Minority Group Adolescents in the United States.* Baltimore: Williams & Wilkins.

Young, Jared J.
1977   *Discrimination, Income, Human Capital Investment, and Asian-Americans.* San Francisco: R & E Research Associates.

Addenda

Myers, Jerome K.
1949   The Differential Time Factor in Assimilation. Unpublished dissertation, Yale University.
1950   "Assimilation to the ecological and social systems of a community." *American Sociological Review* 15 (June):367-372.

Nakane, Chie
1970   *Japanese Society.* Berkeley and Los Angeles: University of California Press.

Nisbet, Robert
1953   *The Quest for Community.* New York: Oxford University Press.
1967   *The Sociological Tradition.* New York: Basic Books.
1973   *The Social Philosophers: Community and Conflict in Western Thought.* New York: Crowell.